# The History of Horfield Parish

## Andy Buchan

# Acknowledgements

My thanks are due to many people and organisations for help and advice and for allowing me to copy and publish documents. Without them this book would not have been possible. These include Bristol Record Office, Bristol Reference Library, Lambeth Palace Library, Gloucestershire Archive, Worcestershire Record Office, Canterbury Cathedral Archive and The Horfield PCC who gave me access to their archives and the church itself. I would like to thank Denis Wright for encouragement, help and advice, John Hyde for reading and commenting on various drafts and last but not least Jo, my wife who has heard me talk of "the book" for several years.

Bishopston Horfield & Ashley Down Local History Society – *Publishers*

c/o Horfield Quaker Meeting, 300 Gloucester Road,
Horfield, Bristol, BS7 8PD

Published: 2008

Copyright: Author and Bishopston, Horfield & Ashley Down LHS

ISBN-13: 978-0-9555826-3-9

All rights reserved. No part of this publication may be reproduced, stored in a retrieval system, or transmitted in any form or by any means, electronic, mechanical, photocopying, recording or otherwise, without the prior permission of the publishers.

Front Cover – extract from Benjamin Donne's "Map of the Country 11 miles round the City of Bristol", dated 1769. Courtesy of Bristol's City Museum and Art Gallery

# Introduction

Horfield parish church, now dedicated to The Holy Trinity and St Edmund, but originally dedicated to St Andrew, lies in the parish of Horfield, a suburb in the northern part of Bristol. Until early in the 20$^{th}$ century this parish lay within Gloucestershire.

This book describes the history and development of Horfield Parish Church, Bristol. It is a church that probably has a very long history although at present this cannot be proven and many of the documents relating to even its more recent history are missing. The surviving documents are scattered in archives across the UK. Many of the drawings are very detailed and beautiful, but unfortunately many are also in a very fragile state and part of the purpose of this book is to record these documents. The aim is also to correct some of the errors that have been written in the past, some of which now seem to be accepted as fact and widely quoted.

A description of the church building as it stands today is included as an appendix.

# Contents

| **Chapter** | | **Page** |
|---|---|---|
| 1. | Early History | 7 |
| 2. | The First Enlargement of the 19<sup>th</sup> Century | 18 |
| 3. | The Second Enlargement – 1847 | 27 |
| 4. | The Third Enlargement – 1893 | 40 |
| 5. | The Last Stages | 49 |
| 6. | The Memorials within the Church | 57 |
| 7. | Memorials in the Churchyard | 75 |
| 8. | The Bells | 85 |
| 9. | The Clock | 89 |
| 10. | The Organ | 90 |
| Appendix 1 | Suggested building history of church before 1836 | 92 |
| Appendix 2 | Outline plans of 19<sup>th</sup> and 20<sup>th</sup> building phases | 93 |
| Appendix 3 | 1836 Petition for the first enlargement | 94 |
| Appendix 4 | 1847 Faculty for the second enlargement | 98 |
| Appendix 5 | The church today – a description | 101 |
| Glossary | | 117 |
| References | | 119 |

# 1. Early History

## Documentary Records

The first recorded reference to a church in Horfield is in the *Taxatio Ecclesiastica Angliae et Walliae Auctoritate Papae Nicholai IV*, circa AD1291-1292. A *taxatio* is an assessment for taxation and this *taxatio* is often called the Pope Nicholas IV *taxatio* because the survey was carried out on his orders. For nearly 250 years virtually all ecclesiastical taxation of England and Wales was based on this survey. The taxation gives the valuation plus related details, of the English and Welsh parish churches and prebends assessed in 1291-2[1]. The information in the various documents linked to the taxation is currently being entered into a new database; the work for this was begun at the University of Manchester and is now being continued at the University of Sheffield.

The information given about Horfield is very limited; it names the church as "Capella de Horefeld" and gives its value as £3.6s.8d (£3.33). It shows that Horfield was in the Diocese of Worcester and that its patron was St Augustine's Abbey, Bristol. There is no description of the church. The value ascribed to the church is the lowest valuation of any of the parish churches extant in the immediate area of Gloucestershire at the time.

There is no mention of a church in Domesday Book but very few churches were mentioned in 1086. If there was a church in Horfield at this date it was probably a wooden structure.

Horfield was in the Berkeley hundred. Taylor[2] says that the hundred was most probably formed after 883 AD and before 1086 AD from a remnant of the estates of the former minster at Berkeley which had reverted to the king. Several authors, including Dawson[3] say that the area was then served by a mother church at Almondsbury and three chapelries at Elberton, Filton, and Horfield. Horfield remained a chapelry of Almondsbury even after it was endowed to St Augustine's

Abbey since there is reference to Almondsbury with its chapels of Elberton and Horfield in 1393[4].

Horfield was included in the lands that Robert Fitzharding, who had been granted the Berkeley estate by Henry II, gave to St Augustine's Abbey on Easter day 1148, the day it was consecrated. On that day Fitzharding who had founded the abbey in 1140 laid upon the high altar his deed of gift by which he endowed it with many manors and lands, including Almondsbury and several other properties. The endowment was of gifts of Domesday berewicks (or part berewicks) belonging to Berkeley. A berewick was an outlying property of an estate and the boundary of the berewick and the boundary of the religious parish of the same name would not necessarily have been the same. The Domesday berewick of Horfield had included the whole of Horfield and Filton, but the endowment covered the whole of Horfield and only a part of Filton.

The next known reference to Horfield dates to 1473 and records the resolution of a dispute between the parishes of Horfield and Filton by John Carpenter, Bishop of Worcester[5]. This document says that Horfield was a dependency of Almondsbury; the dispute related to Filton's right to collect tithes on land and property called Brewesholde in Horfield; but its precise location was not described and it has not proved possible to identify where in the parish this lay.

1.1 Extract from document of 1473
*...proprietorios ecclesie parochialis de Almondesbury cum capella de Horfelde ab eadem dependente et ad ipsam pertinente ex una parte...*

...owners of the parish church of Almondsbury with the chapel of Horfield dependent on the same and appurtenant to the same of the one part...

In 1502 in the will of John Walter of Bristol (Fig 1.2), an important piece in the early story of the church is given, namely that the church was originally dedicated to St Andrew[6]. In his will, John Walter asks "to be buried within the church of St. Andrew of Horefelde". The will also gives the name of the curate and also to whom certain monies should go. This document is considered unusual because it actually gives the dedication for the church. Most documents of this time or any other time simply name the parish.

1.2 Extract from John Walter's will of 1502; the second line above reads

...*corpus qu'meum septiendum infra ecclsiam sancti Andree de Horfelde*...

...*my body is to be buried within the church of Saint Andrew of Horfield*...

When Horfield changed from being a chapelry of Almondsbury to being a parish in its own right is not known, but clearly John Walter considered that he was being buried in a church not a chapel, served by a curate, William Grekeland. Also, the earliest registers for Horfield, which are dated 1543, refer to the "Parishe of Horfilde".

The next official document that might have been expected to mention the church was the *Valor Ecclesiasticus*. This was a survey carried out in 1535, on the orders of Henry VIII, of all religious houses, their estates and holdings. Ostensibly, the purpose of the survey was to ensure that the assessment of First Fruits and Tenths was accurate. These were the annual payments made by churches to the Church. However, the *Valor* was in fact a means to assess the wealth of religious houses and their estates prior to the dissolution of the monasteries. While Almondsbury, Filton and Elberton amongst other churches are listed, Horfield is not included, either in the original document or in the printed text[7, 8]. Other churches were missed, including St Augustine's Abbey but these are known to have been recorded in other related documents of the time[9].

In the succeeding decades the reformation occurred and Horfield became first part of the diocese of Gloucester in 1541 and then part of the diocese of Bristol when this was founded in 1542.

Until, the 19$^{th}$ century few other documents survive. Those that do mainly refer to people associated with the church or in some cases to church business (eg churchwardens' accounts) but they give little detail about the building or any of the related structures.

**The Building**

The church stands at OS reference ST5908976775 on the ridge of high ground that runs through the parish, with fine views to the East and the West.

The Reverend Samuel Seyer, Perpetual Curate of Horfield from 1813-1828, says that the church yard was completely round and this is shown in a sketch map of Horfield that he drew[10] (Fig 1.3); the surveyed plan of the location for the first rectory, which was drawn in 1824[11], shows the shape to be slightly more elliptical, 'pointing' approximately North South (Fig 1.4). The tithe map[12], shows a still less round shape (Fig 1.5). This is probably in part due to the encroachment of the first school in Horfield on the North side, which although built in 1837[13] is not shown on the tithe map, and a widening of the road that ran past the Eastern side of the grave yard. Later maps, including the 1881 OS map (Fig 1.6) and a modern aerial photograph (Fig 1.7), show an even less round area; this is in part due to incorporation on the South East side of a piece of land shown adjacent to the graveyard on the tithe map, Field 88. The North East side of the graveyard is circular and has an outer ditch with a bank on the inside and a hedge growing on the bank (Fig 1.8); it is not known what the original extent of these features was. A count of the tree species within the hedge on the bank suggests that it is probably only 200 or 300 years old. Manorial records show that it was the responsibility of parishioners to maintain the bounds around the church. It is highly probable that the church would have been protected by at least a hedge if not a bank and hedge, if only to keep cattle and sheep grazing on the common out of the graveyard. Seyer in 1824 mentions this problem in relation to the new rectory plot. He wrote on a plan

"………I made a hedge & ditch round it & protected them with post & rails. This was found insufficient against the cattle of the common; & beside in the course of a year the posts and rails gradually disappeared. A stone fence is the only security………………"[14]

Circular graveyards are often said to be an indication that a site may have ancient origins, being the location of an early Christian church on a previous pagan site, Iron-Age or Romano-British. There are some sites in England and Wales that appear to support this idea. Certainly the church's location fits this type of site, being on the highest ground in the parish. However, while a small amount of Romano-British pottery has been found in the area, there is no archaeological evidence to suggest that there were any structures or buildings. Early Christian churches often had circular graveyards and it is probable that there was at least a late Saxon church on the current site. Dawson[3] says the church would appear to have been planted in unenclosed land, ie on land that had not been enclosed/included in a settlement or covered by some form of early estate management.

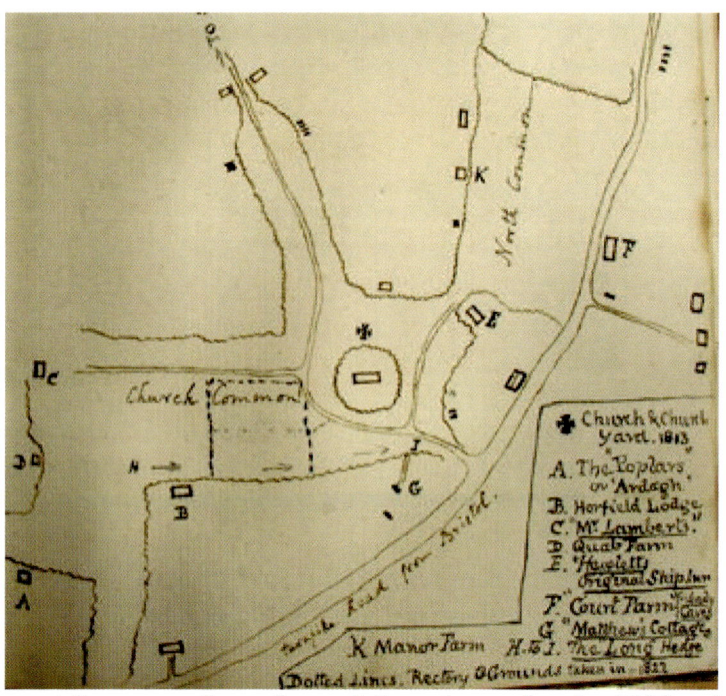

1.3  Extract from map from Samuel Seyer's notebook c1812, with later annotation by Fanshawe Bingham

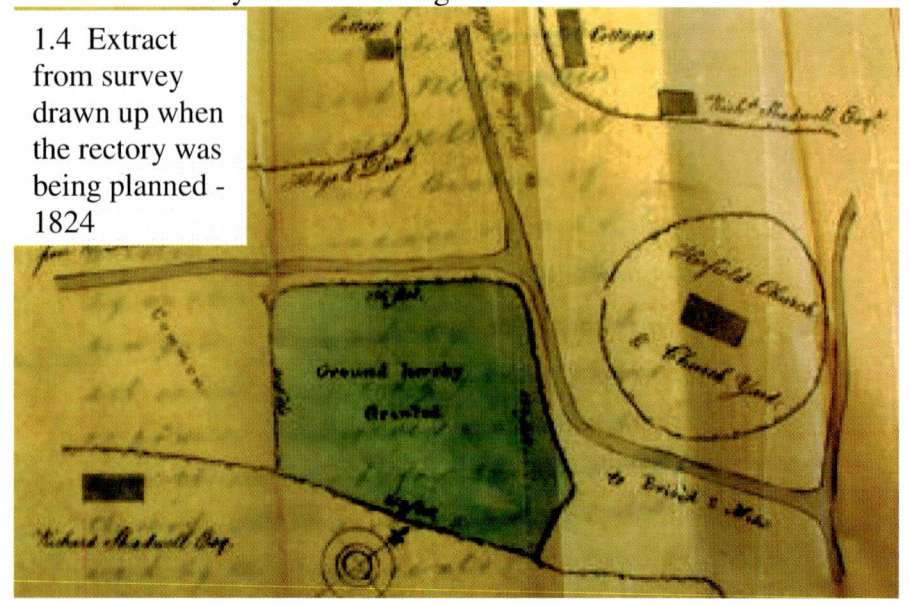

1.4  Extract from survey drawn up when the rectory was being planned - 1824

1.5  Extract from tithe map – 1843

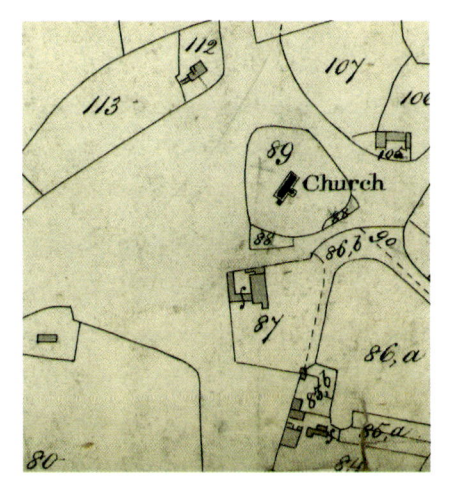

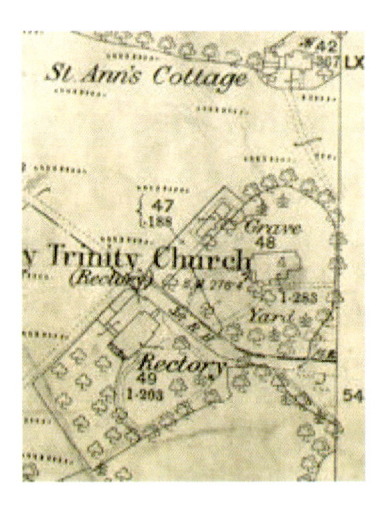

1.6  Reproduced from 1881 Ordnance Survey map with the kind permission of the Ordnance Survey

1.7  Aerial photograph of the church and its surrounding graveyard

1.8 Ditch and inner bank topped by hedge on north side of graveyard

We know very little of the history of the church building that existed before the first major enlargement and rebuild in 1836. What we are able to suggest is based on a drawing of the church as it existed before 1836[13] (Fig 1.9), the current church, and one or possibly two pieces of carved masonry said to be from the original church. The application for funds for the first enlargement of the church in 1836 (see below) says that the church was built of stone in 1530 and that the tower was built in c 1300, but clearly as is explained below these dates must be incorrect.

The drawing shows a small church consisting of a chancel, a nave with a porch on the south side, and a tower at the West end of the nave. Within the church is a piece of carved masonry, which has been in the church since the 19$^{th}$ century (1.10). This is a Romanesque round scalloped capital. Capitals of this design are common throughout the first half of the twelfth century and began to disappear in the later part of the twelfth century. The origin of this capital is not known but Bingham[13] suggests that it is all that remains of the church that was here in 1836. Intriguingly there is a coloured slide, of what may be a second capital from Horfield; the slide (dated 4/1/75) appears to show a very similar capital, which looks as though it has recently been removed from the ground, in the churchyard at Horfield[15]. It may be the same capital but there is no record of the original having been removed from the church. The whereabouts of the capital in the photograph is unknown.

If the capital is from a small early stone church in Horfield, the next development occurred in the 13$^{th}$ century, probably in the first half, with the building of a chancel with a pair of lancet windows, in the Early English style at the East end. That the building of the chancel was a separate later event is suggested by the drawing of the church which shows a definite break in the roofline between the nave and the chancel. The adding of the chancel would probably have increased the length of the church significantly and the additional windows would have let more light into what would formerly have been a small dark interior. It is also possible that the porch was added at this time.

At some point in the late 13$^{th}$- mid 14$^{th}$ century, some coloured window glass was put in one or more windows. This is known from a single coloured drawing made in 1850 by C.Winston, which is shown on the *Corpus Vitrearum Medii Aevi* web-site[42] (Fig 1.11), and the drawing is in the British Library. Where this glass is today is not known.

The final stage in the building of the early church occurred in the 15$^{th}$ century when the tower, which is built in the Perpendicular style with diagonal buttresses, was added. The date 1612 (Fig 1.12) is cut into the South West buttress but the tower is clearly older than the 17$^{th}$ century.

The other information that we can gain about the construction of the early church comes from the architect's plans and notes for the 1836 enlargement (see Chapter 2). The notes record that the roof was built of stone and that the rafters were made of oak. It is likely that by stone the author meant Lias limestone shingles. It is probable that the whole church was built of Lias limestone, much as the tower is.

Apart from occasional tiny pieces of information, there appear to be few documentary records of what happened to the church before the 19$^{th}$ century. For example there is no mention of the hanging or possibly re-hanging of the bells in the late 18$^{th}$ century. There do not appear to be any records of visits and the only correspondence relates to how poor the parish was, a point which Henry Richards in his applications to the ICBS for building funds took pains to make clear. Seyer in his note book[10], mentions new pews being installed in 1764, which was long before he was installed in 1813 and says that these replaced seats with backs in the 'old fashion'. He also says that the Bishop of Bristol, John Kaye, visited the church on the 14$^{th}$ August 1822. He says that the bishop

"……found fault with the state of the churchyard, but approved all things besides."

1.9 Drawing of church before it was rebuilt in 1836

1.10 Romanesque round scalloped capital. This stands in the south transept. The true origin of this capital is unknown.

1.11 A painting of a glass quarry late $13^{th}$- mid $14^{th}$ century. (c) British Library Board. All Rights Reserved Add MS 35211, I f.148. This was found *in situ* in 1850

1.12 The date 1612 is carved into the south west buttress of the tower. However, the tower is significantly older than this.

## 2. The First Enlargement of the 19th Century

During the 19th century the church underwent three phases of expansion aimed at providing accommodation for the increasing population of Horfield. These were intertwined with other building works which were also aimed at increasing the workable space within the church. The increase in the population of Horfield is described in Population in Horfield 1066-1851[15] and was a result of Horfield's expansion to meet the needs for housing the growing workforce of Bristol.

Bingham[13] says that the first major enlargement of Horfield parish church took place in 1831 and that a licence or faculty for the work was not applied for from the Bishop of Bristol until 1836 - a story that has been retold by others. Examination of the records shows this to be incorrect. A substantial repair was carried out in 1828[16], at a cost of £68 (Fig 2.2), but no details are known, and there is no record of any work to enlarge the church before 1836. Examination of records held at Lambeth Palace of the Incorporated Church Building Society (ICBS)[16], an organisation founded in 1818 to provide funds for the building and enlargement of Anglican churches in England and Wales, shows that early in February 1836 Henry Richards, the Incumbent, contacted the society asking if there was an act of parliament to enable a church to be built on copyhold land held under a bishop. He explained that the church was too far from the population which was increasing daily along with the population of the parish. He said that he had no power to build a chapel unless there was power under some act that would force the bishop to make it freehold. Clearly at this time Richards was not thinking about expanding Horfield parish church but was proposing to build a new church near to where the main population of Horfield was living, possibly in the area on which St Michael & All Angels church stood until recently.

In March 1836 correspondence from Richards suggests that he had sent two sets of plans for the new church to the ICBS, one for a large rectangular church and the other for a cruciform shaped church. The architect chosen was John Hicks of Bristol. Later correspondence shows that he decided against the rectangular shape, which he later adopted in 1847, and also that the area of the chancel should be reduced to give more space in the nave.

Richards's original reason for writing to the ICBS was to obtain funds towards the building of the new church. However, by late March of 1836 it must have been clear to Richards that he would not be able to raise sufficient funds from any source to build a new church and an application was submitted for the enlargement of Horfield parish church. The problem in raising sufficient funds is confirmed in an advertisement in Felix Farley's Journal for 14$^{th}$ May 1836 asking for more people to subscribe money to the enlargement of the existing church (Fig 2.4). Eventually, £500 was raised by subscription and the ICBS eventually gave £130, after initially promising £100. The main remit of the ICBS was to enable more people to attend church. It was therefore important that the plans for the enlargement clearly show how many extra people the enlarged church would be able to accommodate. For this reason, early plans show that entry to the enlarged church would be through a door in the South wall of the new South transept, but later plans show that a door would be inserted into the West wall of the base of the tower. Moving the door meant extra seating could be put in the transept. Even the eventual need to rebuild much of the church (see below), which meant that the eventual cost was nearer £700 than the projected £400, was reported as meaning that a further thirty additional sittings could be installed.

The ICBS Minute books and associated correspondence chart the progress of the work from the approval of the plans in April 1836, through the discovery of the parlous condition of much of the fabric in late 1836, to the certificate of completion sent on 11$^{th}$ January 1837, albeit that while two coats of paint had been applied to the walls two further coats of paint would need to be applied in the Spring and Summer of that year. The ICBS grant was only to be paid upon completion of the work and Richards was concerned, especially since the work was already over budget, that the ICBS would not pay the money out until all the work had been completed; in the event the money was paid on 3rd February 1837.

It is unclear why Bingham thought that the first enlargement was carried out in 1831, when it was actually carried out in 1836. It is clear from the application for funds to the ICBS that the requirement for a faculty was known (Fig 2.3). The petition for the faculty was raised well after work had begun. The petition actually asked the bishop to allow the work that had been carried out to remain rather than asking for permission to carry out the work, this was probably before 15th November 1836 when the Bishop wrote to the ICBS recommending that the request be given favourable consideration, which was some two months before the certificate of completion was sent to the ICBS. That the wider church had to have known what was going on before the petition was submitted is shown by the fact that in both the first application to the ICBS in March 1836 (Fig 2.1) and the revised application in April 1836 Henry Richards states that the plan, specification and estimate had been submitted to the Rural Dean, R G Bedford because there was no Archdeacon. The application also says that a faculty had not yet been obtained. Given that when the faculty was eventually applied for it was written out very fully and in the correct format/style for the time it looks as though the failure to apply was an oversight and that everyone concerned suddenly woke up to the fact when it was not just a few walls being taken down but effectively the whole church being demolished and re-built. This also involved disruption/movement of graves and memorials. In the Felix Farley Journal of 12th November 1836[20], it says that the church is to reopen on the Sunday, ie 13th November, but on the 23rd November Richard's wrote to the ICBS informing them of the poor state of the fabric which meant that most of the church would have to come down, excluding the tower. The certificate of completion was not actually submitted until the 11th January 1837 and it is not clear if the report in the journal is inaccurate or if some form of service was able to be held.

Between the application to the ICBS and the petition[17] (see Appendix 3) we are able to learn a lot of information both about the size and layout of the early church and about details of the enlarged church, especially its size, layout and number of sittings. Of the old church, crucially we learn the size internally. The nave was 37.5 feet (11.43m) long, 16.25 feet (4.95m) wide and 20.5 feet (6.25m) high, while the chancel was 23.5 feet (7.16m) long. The total length of the church was thus 61 feet (18.59m). The initial plan had been to demolish the North and South walls of the chancel, leaving the East wall standing, together with sections of the North and South nave walls, and then build two new transepts. The plan also called for the installation of galleries in the transepts, across the West end of the nave and in the tower, to give extra seating within the footprint of the original church.

In fact what happened was that when the roof was removed it was found to be in such a ruinous condition that it could not be re-used. The North wall of the chancel was near collapse, because of problems with the foundations, and structurally the other walls were in such poor condition that the architect advised that all but the tower and the west wall of the nave should be pulled down and the whole church rebuilt. It is not clear why the walls were in such poor condition. Other later documents show that clearly later builders had known of problems with the clay sub-soil, but in 1836 the thickness of the walls must have been considered significant because in the faculty it says that the walls were to be built of stone and that they were to be 2.5 feet (0.76m) thick. How long the work took to complete is not known, but it is likely to have been a great deal longer than the one week, which Richards stated in his original application to the ICBS.

The internal dimensions of the new church are reported as being 61.5 feet (18.74m) long, total length of nave and chancel, with a width of 16.25 feet (4.95m). The church was to have two wings or transepts each to project twelve feet (3.66m) clear and to be 16 feet (4.88m) wide. It is interesting that even in the early plans for the enlargement when it was planned that entry to the church would be through the South transept, the decision had been taken to remove the porch and doorway into the nave and insert a window in its place, which would have required more work to the South wall of the nave than is otherwise mentioned. Ultimately, the decision was taken to make a doorway through the base of the tower.

The petition also describes at length the seating and other arrangements within the church. There was to be a vestry room on the ground floor of the North Transept, four pews, and a flight of stairs to a gallery holding nine pews. The South transept was to have eight pews on the ground floor and a flight of stairs to a gallery containing nine pews. Finally across the full width of the nave at its westward end was to be another gallery, which was to extend into the tower. The effect of all the additional seating was to increase the capacity of the church from 65, for a population of "nearly 630" to 237 of which 130 were free sittings. Some have doubted as to whether the galleries were ever actually installed but Joseph Leach in his Rural Rides or Calls at Country Churches column in the Bristol Times in May 1845[20], published in book form in 1850[18] describes the church as follows:

> "The church is a neat, but small structure, being if I may use the expression, a miniature cruciform building, having nave, cross aisles and chancel. There is a pretty east window and some painted glass…………………………….."
>
> "In the cross aisles are small galleries, and the Church in other respects has rather a crowded appearance, the pulpit and reading desk interrupting the view of the altar."

Further on in the same article he mentions "In a pew immediately below me, (for I sat in the gallery)……………………." He also says that this was in the "churchwarden's pew."

The petition also describes where the reading desk was to be placed and also gave assurance to the bishop that the tablets and memorials removed as part of the building work had been preserved and had been replaced as near as possible to their original locations. What is not made clear is what happened to graves and gravestones that must have been disturbed when the transepts were built. The 1847 petition, as we will see later, was also not clear about exactly what happened to disturbed graves.

2.1 The cover from one of Henry Richard's applications to the ICBS in 1836 for funds to enlarge Horfield Church; this one is dated 25th March 1836. A second one is known which is dated 23rd April 1836

2.2 Page one of the March 1836 application to the ICBS, this says in answer to question 4 that the church was last "substantially repaired" in 1828.

2.3 Page two of the same application.
In answer to question 13 it says that the Rural Dean has been told of the plans.
In answer to question 14, which asks if a faculty has been applied for it says "not yet been obtained"; implying that it was known one would be needed.

2.4 A public appeal for funds for the enlargement work of Horfield church in Felix Farley's Journal dated 14th May 1836.

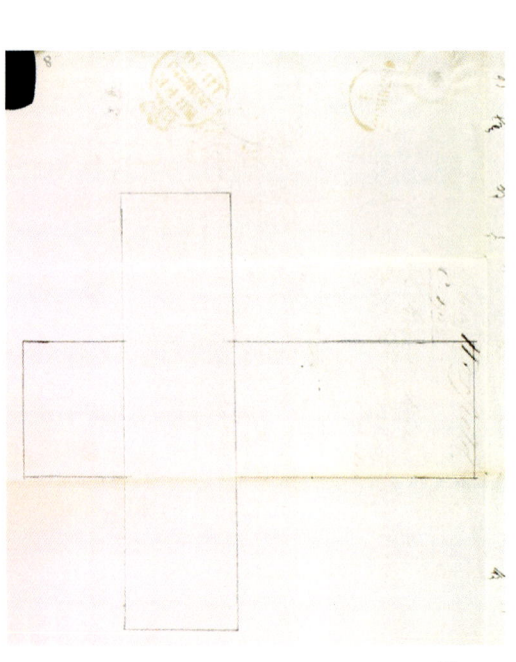

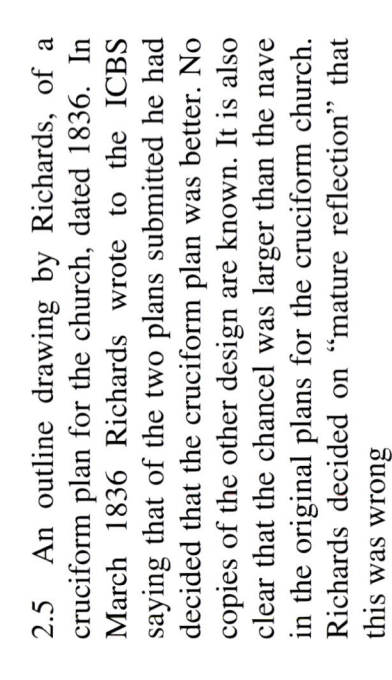

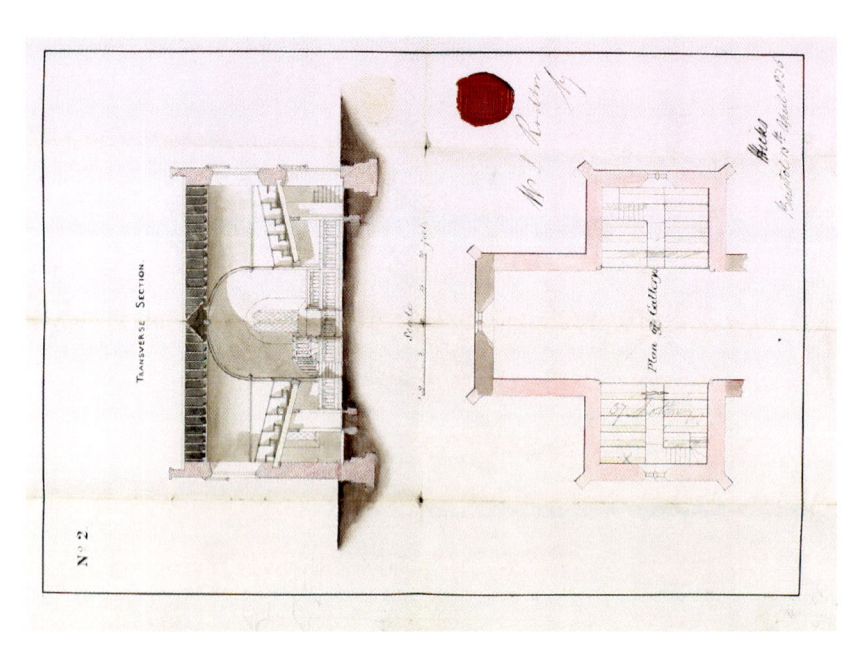

2.6 Early architect's drawing showing how the chancel might look.

2.5 An outline drawing by Richards, of a cruciform plan for the church, dated 1836. In March 1836 Richards wrote to the ICBS saying that of the two plans submitted he had decided that the cruciform plan was better. No copies of the other design are known. It is also clear that the chancel was larger than the nave in the original plans for the cruciform church. Richards decided on "mature reflection" that this was wrong

24

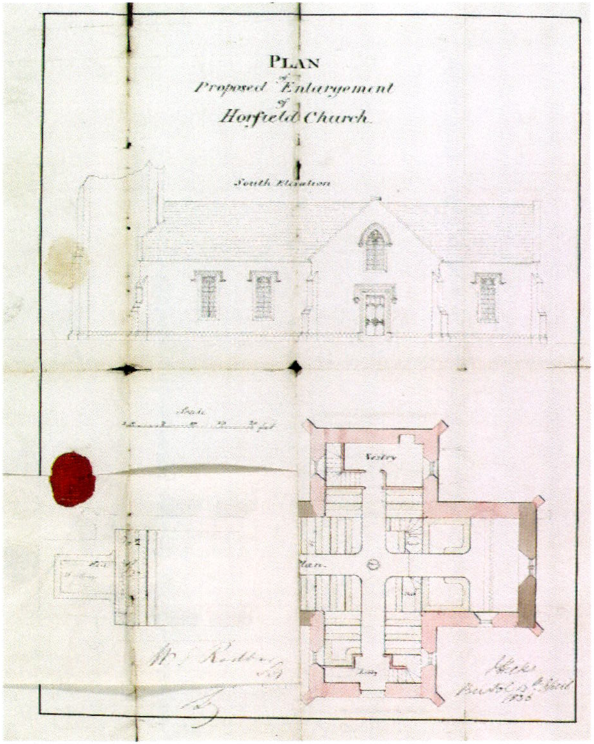

2.7 Early architect's drawing, with a mask over the nave, showing new transepts and also how the South side of new church would look; also seating on first floor of tower. New walls are shown in pink.

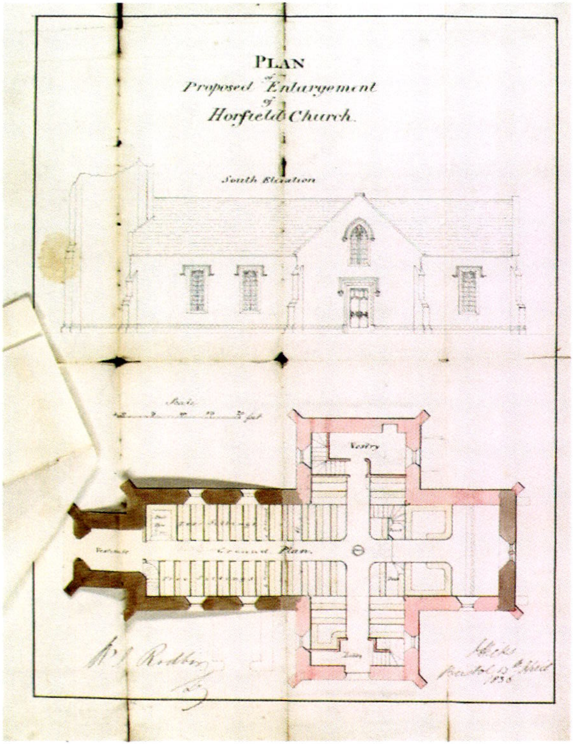

2.8 Same plan, but with mask over nave removed. This shows the nave untouched and the new door through tower.

25

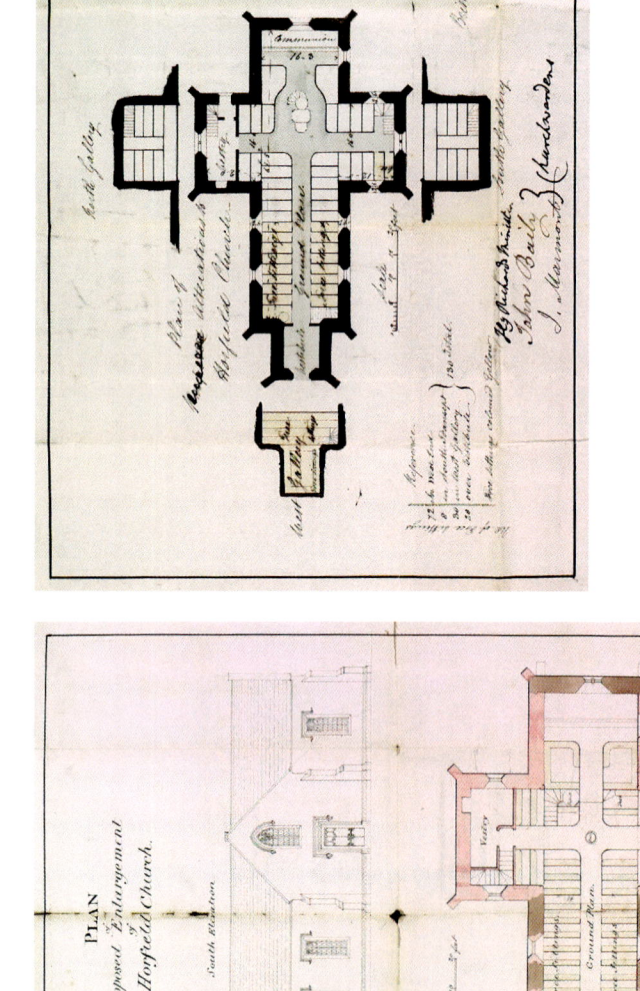

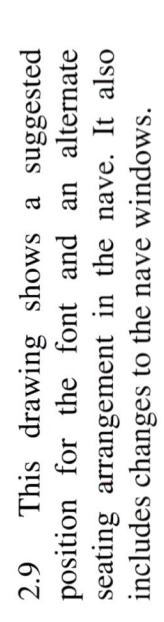

2.10 The date of this ground-plan, November 1836, means that it is very likely that this is a drawing of the actual ground-plan of the 1836 church.

2.9 This drawing shows a suggested position for the font and an alternate seating arrangement in the nave. It also includes changes to the nave windows.

26

## 3. The Second Enlargement

The second enlargement of the church occurred in 1847, and was a result of the increasing population of Horfield, which by this time had nearly trebled from the 328 quoted in the 1831 census; in 1851 the census recorded a population of 998. In addition a new barracks had been built in Horfield, close to the common in 1847, which was not to get its own chapel until 1857.

The enlargement was also needed because the seating arrangements installed in 1836 had not been successful; Henry Richards reported to the ICBS in November 1847[19] that the arrangement of the seating in the galleries had been poor and that some seats had been unusable; in essence there had proved to be a real difference between the theoretical number of sittings and the number of people who could practically be seated. This was the reason that the galleries had been removed during the latest building work. Richards also reported that they were having to use the vestry for seating and that because the church was so cold in Winter some seating had had to be sacrificed for a stove and heating. Furthermore, in the tower gallery consideration had not been given for the space required for the bell ropes and clock weights etc, which also made the seating unsafe for children. Some of these observations are interesting because in at least one of the plans for the 1836 building work a stove is shown on the plan positioned at the crossing.

The petition for the faculty[21] for the work was presented to the Bishop in October 1846. The work was to be carried out in two parts. The chancel was to be lengthened and two windows and a door were to be installed in the South wall. In the North wall there was to be one window and a door leading to a new vestry to be built on the North side of the chancel. A chancel screen was to be erected and the pulpit and reading desk were to be re-positioned from the centre of the church to either side of the aisle leading to the altar. This would also resolve the complaint mentioned by Joseph Leach that the central position of the pulpit and reading desk hindered the view of the altar.

The second part of this work was to increase the capacity of the nave by extending the walls of the nave from the ends of the transepts down towards the tower, knocking down the old nave walls and replacing them with pillars to support the roof, thus creating North and South aisles either side of the nave. The plan also included building a new entrance to the church through the new wall of the South aisle together with a new porch. The work would also involve arching over four graves that were close to the eastern wall of the chancel. There is no mention of what was to happen to other graves, monuments or tablets within the church, which might be affected by the work, in contrast to the 1836 petition. The faculty (Appendix 4) says that finance for the work was to be raised by subscription and that there should not be any need to increase the church rate. This is not entirely true because some funds were obtained from the ICBS. It was anticipated that the enlargement of the church would increase the accommodation from c 200 to c 340. There are many plans and also drawings of how the enlarged church should look. Some show the new vestry to be at the East end of the North wall of the chancel, while others show it at the western end of the North wall abutting onto the East wall of the North aisle. Similarly, one of the plans shows a 'heating room' on the North side of the tower. There is no indication that the heating room was built and it is not possible to be sure of the location of the new vestry. Later drawings or plans do not offer any clues. The numbers of windows on the North side also differ in different plans/drawings.

It is widely reported that the design for the 1847 re-build was by the celebrated architect William Butterfield, who was clearly active in the Bristol area at the time; but while certain aspects of the design including the altar cloth, may be attributed to him there is nothing on any of the drawings to suggest that Butterfield was involved. In fact almost all the plans and drawings are un-signed, which is in contrast to the plans for most of the other building works carried out on the church.

The petition also asked if, because of the significant amount of building work involved, consideration be given to a service of re-consecration. The Church decided that this question should be left to the bishop at a later time.

An interesting point linked to the proposed changes to the church is confusion over the name. In both an ICBS record[19] and in the article in Felix Farley's Journal[20] about the re-opening of the chancel, the church is referred to as St Michaels and, as reported in the article mentioned above, and described below in detail, a large painted window of St Michael triumphing over a dragon had been installed in the church. The name does not appear in the faculty or a second but related faculty for the re-consecration of the church. Eventually Richard's used the dedication for the first parish church in Bishopston, which was called St Michael and All Angels.

Unlike the petition for the 1836 enlargement, the petition for the 1847 enlargement does not give details of the dimensions of the new church. Fortunately this information is given by Bingham who says that the nave was 48 feet (14.63m) long by 40 feet (12.19m) wide and the chancel was 24 feet (7.32m) long and 16.5 feet (5.03m) wide[13]. After the 1847 building work had been completed, only the tower would remain from the pre 19th century church.

It is not known how soon after the faculty was granted that work began, but by early February 1847, the work on the new chancel had been completed and the galleries had been removed from the nave; in Felix Farley's Journal dated 13th February 1847[20] the church was described as follows:

"The chancel of St Michael's Church, Horfield, near this city, having through the exertions of the Incumbent, the Rev. Henry Richards, recently been rebuilt and fitted up with stained glass windows, was re-opened for divine service on Thursday last [11th February ].

The east window, and the two windows on the south side of the chancel, are by Mr M. O'Connor, of Berners-street London, formerly of Bristol, and represent the principal events in the life of our Lord, from the Nativity to the Ascension.

There is also a window of painted glass in the west end of the church, by [Joseph] Bell, of Bristol, representing St. Michael (to whom the church is dedicated) triumphing over the dragon; this subject is comprised in one light, and in the other is the Annunciation. The addition of these painted windows gives a solemn appearance to the interior of the church.

The chancel has been entirely rebuilt in the decorated style; formerly it was in what is called the debased style. The floor of the chancel and the altar are laid with encaustic tiles from Messrs. Minton's of Stoke-upon-Trent. On the south side of the chancel, are the piscina and sedilid (*sic*); and in the centre of the chancel, the lectern. The altar is covered with rich green silk, with gold *fleur-de-lis* and stars, designed by Mr. Butterfield of London. We understand that the whole of the ornamental work was presented to the Incumbent. The unsightly galleries have been removed, but by throwing open the vestry nearly the same number of sittings have been preserved."

It is not known precisely when work on the enlargement of the nave began. According to Bingham, the walls of the new nave were erected around the old church, so that services might continue. Bingham goes on to say that the last of the services was held in the old building on the 5th September 1847 and that on the 9th September the foundation stone of the new building was laid by Robert B. Hale Esq., M.P. for South Gloucestershire from 1836 to 1857. But once work began on the final stage of the enlargement the congregation was restricted to parishioners only and services were held in the chancel.

In December 1847, Richards applied for a faculty to have a service of re-consecration and ask that the church be re-dedicated[22]. While to whom the church is to be dedicated is not mentioned in the faculty, it is mentioned elsewhere in diocesan records that the church was to be dedicated to the Holy Trinity[23]. The service of re-consecration took place on December 22nd 1847 and was reported in Felix Farley's Journal on 25th December 1847[20]. The newspaper article says that the builder of the church was a Mr Robertson of Stokes Croft, Bristol. The article describes the completed church as follows:

> "The church has been enlarged to the extent of the former transepts, and now consists of a chancel, nave, and north and south aisles. On the south side a very elegant porch has been erected, which adds greatly to the appearance of the building. The aisles are laid with encaustic tiles, placed lozenge-way; the seats are oak, low and open, forming a striking contrast to the former ugly pews. The roof is of oak, and open and rests upon stone pillars and arches. The east and west windows, and the windows on the south side, are of stained glass, and we suppose the windows on the north side will, as soon as possible, be made to correspond with the others. Altogether the Church is a beautiful specimen of ecclesiastical architecture."

The service was clearly a major event and the article lists many of the dignitaries that attended, as well as military personnel from the barracks. Richards, in a letter to the ICBS says that nearly 600 people attended, with 50 children in the chancel.

3.1 An early photograph of the church after the enlargement in 1847

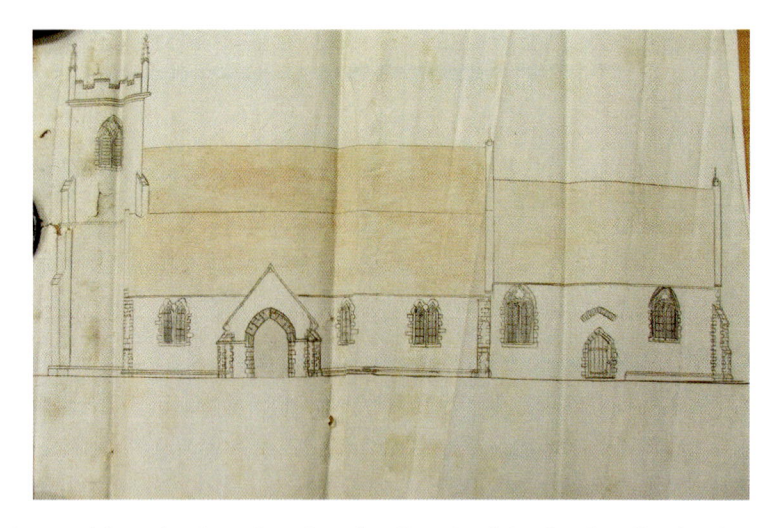

3.2 An architect's drawing for the South side; in the final scheme the porch was moved closer to the tower, there was no window between the porch and the tower and two two-light windows to the East of the porch.

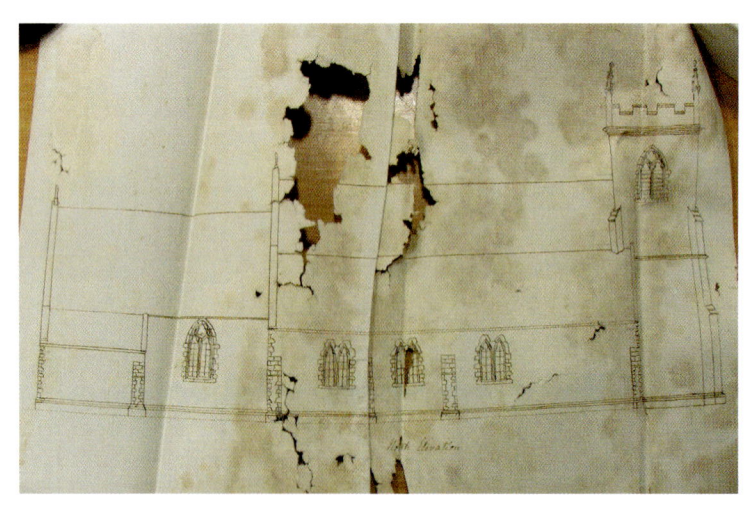

3.3 An architect's drawing for the North side; in the final scheme the nave windows took a slightly different form and it is not known if the window closest to the tower was inserted during this phase. Also the vestry was built further west butting against the North aisle and there was no window inserted in the North wall of the chancel.

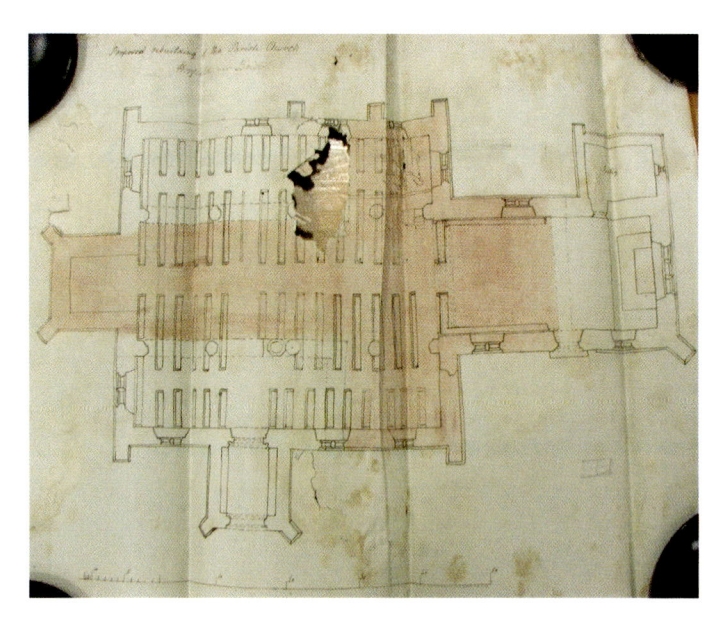

3.4 A ground-plan for the 1847 enlargement, showing the outline of the 1836 church; this plan is linked to the two previous drawings and is not the final ground-plan.

3.5 This ground-plan appears to be close to the final layout of the 1847 re-build.

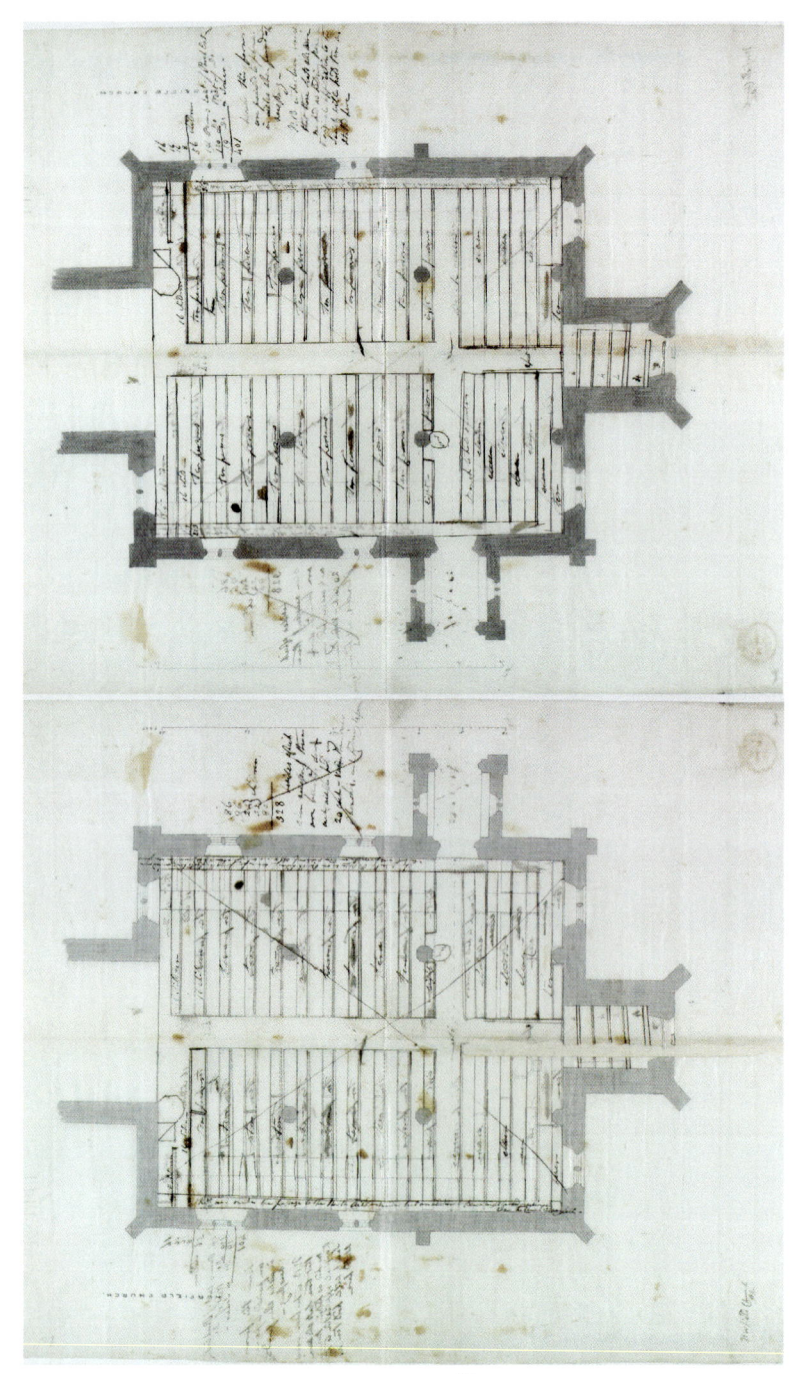

3.6 The front and reverse of the same ground-plan showing different calculations for how many people might be seated in the enlarged church.

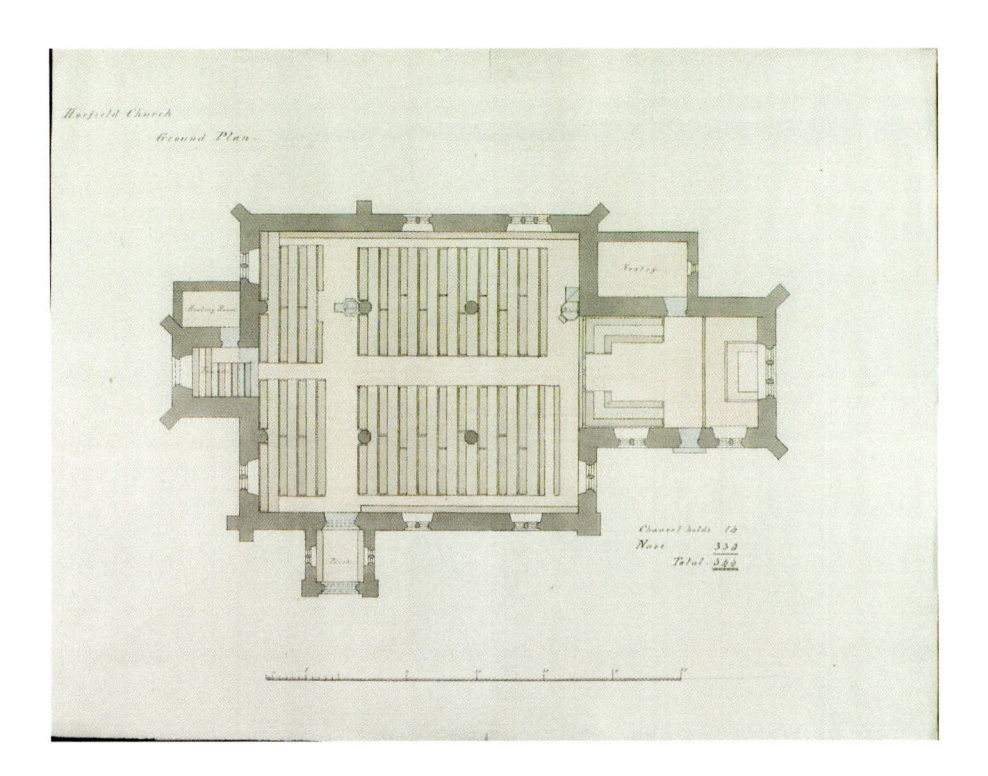

3.7 An alternative ground-plan for the 1847 enlargement; this is similar to what is assumed to be the final plan, except that the plan shows a heating room on the north side of the tower that was never built.

The drawings above show that there must have been a number of different proposals for the design, both in terms of the design of the building and the seating arrangements, but only some of these documents have survived.

Some of these photographs also show the poor condition of a number of the documents that were examined during the preparation of this book.

3.8  A photograph of the church taken in the 1880s before the next phase of enlargement in 1893; it gives a good idea of how the building would have looked after the 1847 enlargement. The photograph must have been taken after 1882 because bats-wing gas lights may be seen around the tops of the capitals. Gas lighting was installed in the church in 1882.

The lower part of the chancel screen is said to be part of the original medieval screen, while the top half is late Victorian having been donated by the Revered Hardy as a memorial to his sisters[24].

The glass in the East window is the same glass that was described in Felix Farley's Journal in 1847, showing the "principal events in the life of our Lord, from the Nativity [on the left] to the Ascension [on the right]".

The next major phase of enlargement did not occur until 1893, but in the intervening period some building works were carried out and other changes made.

In 1864 Henry Richards was succeeded at Horfield by Henry Haistwell Hardy. Until this time, so far as is known, the church was lit solely by candles, which meant that the interior would probably have been fairly dark. In 1865/66, Hardy, soon after his installation, is reported to have installed paraffin oil lamps in place of candles[24]. Hardy is also credited with the insertion of a single clerestory on each of the North and South sides of the nave roof at its eastern end. This assumption is based on photographs dated to the mid 1870s (Fig 3.9). It is not known if the original intention was to install further clerestories later on either side, but this would be a logical conclusion given the position of the extant clerestories. Hardy is also said to have had installed the third, most westerly, window in the North aisle[24]. Stylistically, this window is very similar to the other windows on the North side and, as previously mentioned, different drawings for the 1847 work show differing numbers of windows on the North side. This window is also very similar in all ways to the window at the West end of the South aisle, the only difference being that the glass in the window in the North aisle looks old. It contains ripples and other defects not seen in the window in the South aisle. Unfortunately, there are no known documentary records relating to the work credited to Hardy. While records for these works no longer remain, records for another building plan, which went as far as getting a faculty, are still extant. This was a plan for a new organ chamber and vestry room at the East end of the North aisle. The architect for this work was Henry Crisp, who was to be the architect for the next building phase, ten years later. At least some of the drawings are dated June 1873, but the work was not approved at a vestry meeting until 14th February 1876[26] and the faculty is dated 8th June 1876[25]. It is not known why this work was not carried out.

Hardy was succeeded as Rector of Horfield in 1878 by Fanshaw Bingham who was to oversee the next major building phase at Horfield in the early 1890's. But before then he introduced gas lighting in December 1882[27]. This followed a vestry meeting in November 1882, when it was agreed that gas lighting would be installed as soon as the gas main was close enough to the church. Funds would be raised by voluntary subscription to include the laying of the gas pipe from the main road to the church[28].

3.9 Photograph of the church c1870 after the clerestories were installed.

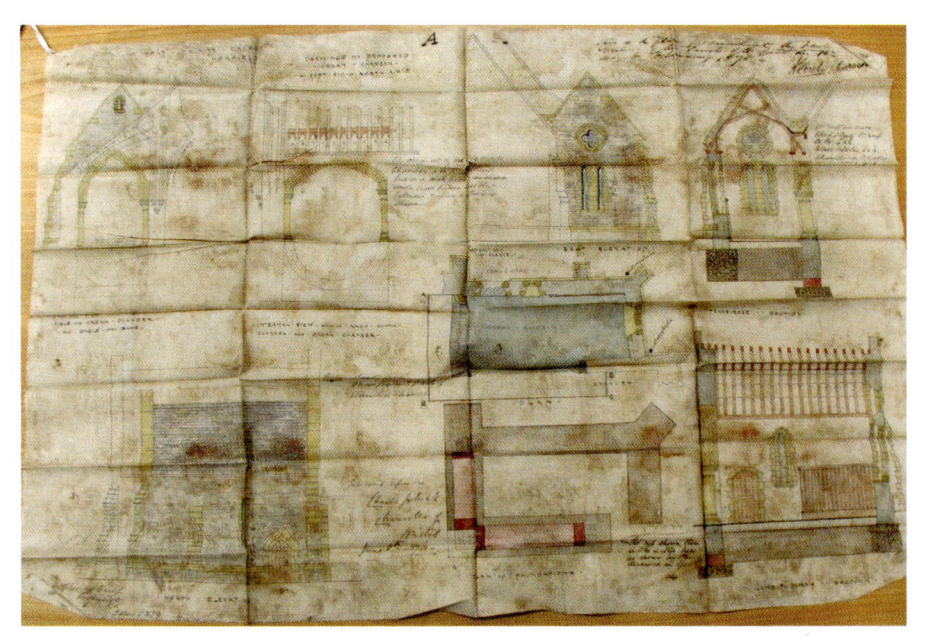

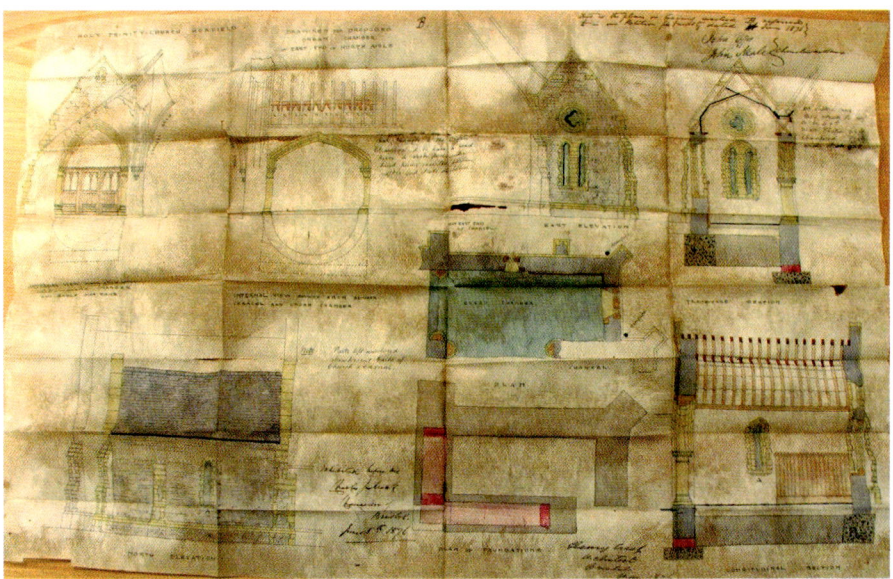

3.10 Drawings A and B for the proposed organ loft; the faculty says that B is the plan that must be followed. This organ loft was not built. Drawing A is on fabric and B is on paper.

## 4. The Third Enlargement

By the beginning of the 1880's it was becoming apparent that plans would have to be made to cope with a still expanding population. In 1881 it had reached 2378, and, as in 1846, initial thoughts were for a second church, this time a mission church, to be built at Golden Hill. A committee was established and various organisations were asked for funding. Unfortunately, for various reasons including potential sponsors not prepared to make funds available or applying unacceptable conditions to their sponsorship, the plan was dropped and a decision was taken to look to enlarging the existing parish church. The plan was that the enlargement would be funded by a combination of subscriptions and private donations.

In 1884, a premium was offered, by advertisement for a plan for enlargement of the church, the sole condition attached being that the medieval tower had to remain, it being the only part of the pre-19$^{th}$ century church still standing. The architect who was eventually chosen was Henry Crisp, the same architect who had some years previously put forward the plans for the organ loft; this would not have been known when his plan was chosen because the plan had been signed "Spero". The plan which was chosen unanimously included transepts and an enlarged chancel; it was later to be modified by the addition of a lantern tower, an idea put forward by Bingham himself[13]. At this time the estimated cost was £1600.

Funds came in very slowly and a decision was taken in 1885, to obtain a new organ to replace the very small "one manual" organ, which had been given by the Reverend Raymond Barker before the enlargement in 1847. This appeal for funds for the organ was more successful; the organ was ordered from Palmer of Bristol in March 1885 and dedicated on the 17$^{th}$ September 1885. This organ albeit modified several times over the years, is still in use today. Full details of the organ, including more details on its history are given in Chapter 10.

A renewed appeal for funds for the enlargement was begun in 1885; the appeal was supported by the Bishop and was sent out accompanied by a poem written by Bingham (Fig 4.1). The money only came in very slowly and so the decision was taken to carry out the work in sections. It was therefore decided to build the tower (choir) vestry to a design drawn up by Henry Crisp (Fig 4.3). This was to be sited at the West end of the North aisle and against the North wall of the tower and the entrance to it was to be from the ground floor of the tower[29]. The building would be a memorial to the 50$^{th}$ year of Queen Victoria's reign. Work began on 7$^{th}$ March 1887 and was completed by September of that year, at a total cost, including fittings, of £194.18s (£194.80). The builder was Messrs. W. Cowlin & Son.

In addition to raising funds for the enlargement money was also needed for other repairs to the fabric of the church, including the bells, and in the same year money was used to pay for the wheels of the church bells to be repaired after they gave way through age on Jubilee Day, 21$^{st}$ June 1887[13].

Bingham[13] describes in detail the problems encountered by the church in raising the necessary funds; including also the later events that were used to raise monies to pay off the costs incurred. One of these was to charge 1d (0.5p), equivalent to 33p today, for the order of service for the re-consecration. In 1893, the estimated cost, excluding the transepts, had risen to £2281. The final cost was to be £2148, 18s 5d (£2148.82). With an ultimatum, that unless the shortfall was found, some of the promised funds would be withdrawn, Bingham obtained the final £600 needed through the combination of a loan of £300, from the Reverend J. R. Radcliffe and an overdraft of £300 from the bank. This would be equivalent to nearly £48,000 today, a significant amount of money. The loan by the Reverend Ratcliffe was cleared by the end of 1896, but the loan by the bank was not finally cleared until just before Bingham left in December 1899 and then only with the financial help of building committee members.

Bingham gives the dimensions, "omitting inches", of the church following completion of the work in 1893, as follows:

"Chancel, 31ft. x 16ft. – (The White Marble Slab in the middle of the Chancel floor, marks the spot where the Altar Table stood from 1847 to 1893.)
Nave, 64ft. x 40ft. of which the Centre Aisle is 48ft. x 16ft.
Side Aisles 48ft. x 12ft.     Lantern Tower 16ft. x 16ft.
Chapel of S. Andrew, 17ft x 12 ft     Vestry, 19ft x 12ft."

Many of the known, signed, drawings and plans are solely signed by Henry Crisp, as architect. It is known that George Oatley, later to be Sir George Oatley who designed the Wills Memorial Tower at Bristol University, assisted on the plans and design, and this probably increased after he became a partner in 1889. Most plans with George Oatley's name on them are dated 1891 or later[30,31]. It is also probable that he took a more active role during the building work stage, because Henry Crisp was in failing health. The Bristol Times & Mirror for 23rd December 1893 in its description of the re-consecration reported that Henry Crisp was unable to attend through illness. Henry Crisp died in 1896. The builders were Messrs. W. Cowlin & Son.

Bingham estimated that the enlarged church would be able to hold 450 people, from a previous capacity of 250. Two things are clear from these accommodation figures, firstly that in 1847 as in 1836, the estimated increased capacity of the enlargements, which was the only reason that the ICBS would give grants, was clearly inaccurate and second that Bingham was clearly a pragmatist in eventually going with the enlargement that he did, given that his original appeal in 1885, included the line "Population 2300, Church Accommodation, only 250!".

The foundation stone of the chancel was laid by Mrs Pigou, wife of the Dean of Bristol, on the 22nd June 1893, more than two years after the faculty had been granted[32], and the completed church, to the reduced plan, ie effectively everything bar the transepts was re-consecrated by the Bishop on the 22nd December 1893[33], this date being the anniversary of the re-consecration in 1847.

## The Rector's Appeal.

Not for my own, but for my people's sake
Grant me the friendly privilege to take
Of asking you—though stranger to our need—
With generous help, our anxious work to speed.
The Work being costly and our Parish Poor,
We're forced to ask for aid at every door.
Hence This Appeal,—We hope 'twill not prove vain,
Which seeks from you some little help to gain.
For though one Parish may not hold us both,
Yet still "One Faith" enrolls us,—nothing loth,
'Neath This far-spreading banner, Who in Love,
The Heavenly Life has brought us from Above.
For His Dear Sake, "Who bare our Sorrows" here,
And took from death its sharpest cause for fear,—
From East to West, from North to South, we plead,
Christ's Kingdom knows no bounds, but those of need.
Wherever man gives help, 'tis God's to Own:
The Cheerful Giver gives to Him alone.
There's nothing lost, the Giver too is blest,
With greater gain than time's short interest.
The thousand souls—perchance unknown to fame,
The countless voices, won to praise God's Name,
By gifts of pious hearts, made One in prayer,
Rich jewels for the Crown of Life prepare.
With grateful thanks, these all will gather there,
Though sea, or land, or time divide them here,—
Where neither sea, nor land, can cast a bar,
Nor Earth's brief strains their endless raptures mar.
"Bis dat qui cito dat," an Author wrote,
Twice happy we, if you this plea will note,
And kindly help with bounteous hand, to raise
Our Temple, meet for Holy Prayer and Praise.

    HORFIELD RECTORY,                      F.B.
        1885

4.1 A copy of Fanshawe Bingham's appeal poem printed in Horfield Miscellanea[13] In his book Bingham says this is "slightly revised" from the version that went out with the appeal.

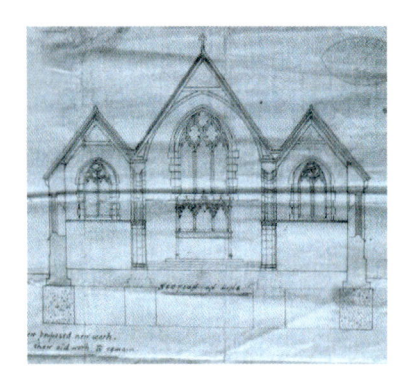

4.2 Part of presumably a series of drawings from 1884-1891 showing how the new enlarged church might look. Notice the second clerestory has been crossed out in the lower drawing. The church today looks similar to the bottom drawing. Note in the drawing there is no clock in the West tower.

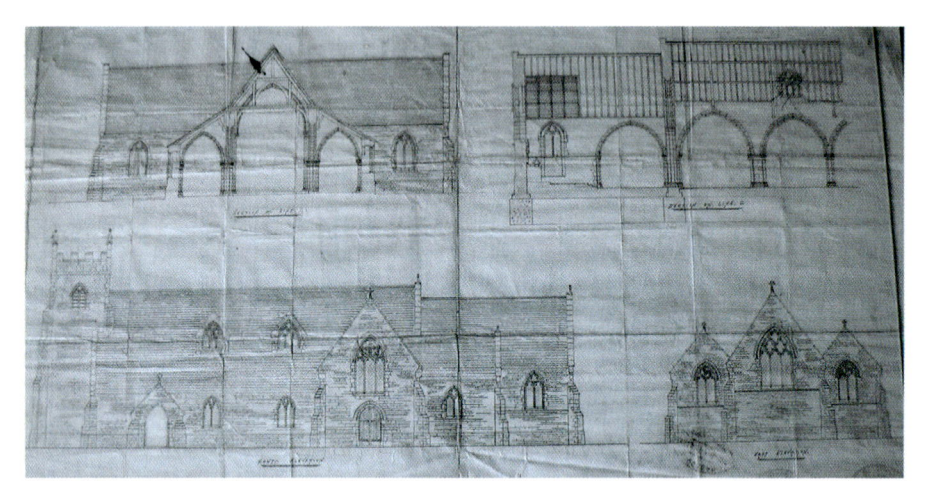

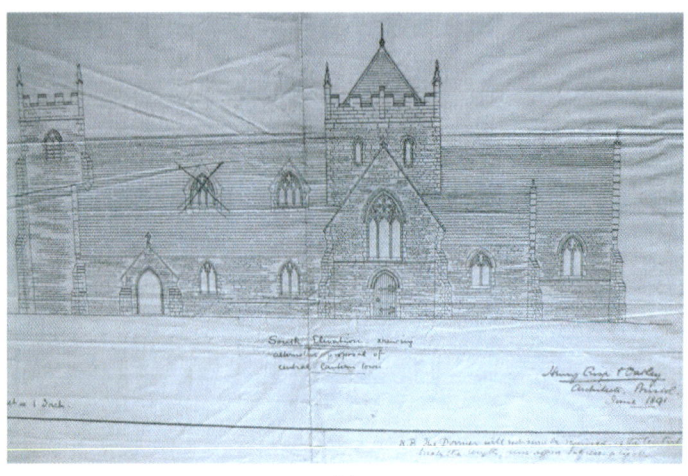

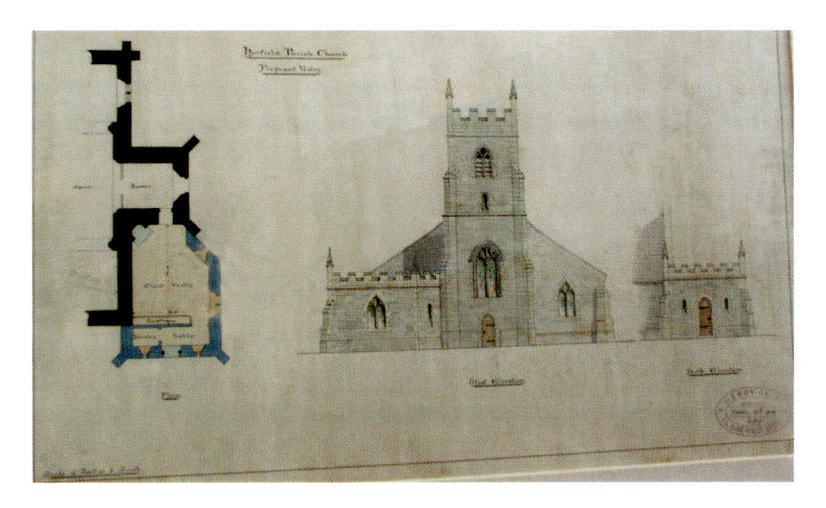

4.3 Ground-plan and drawing for the choir vestry built in 1887

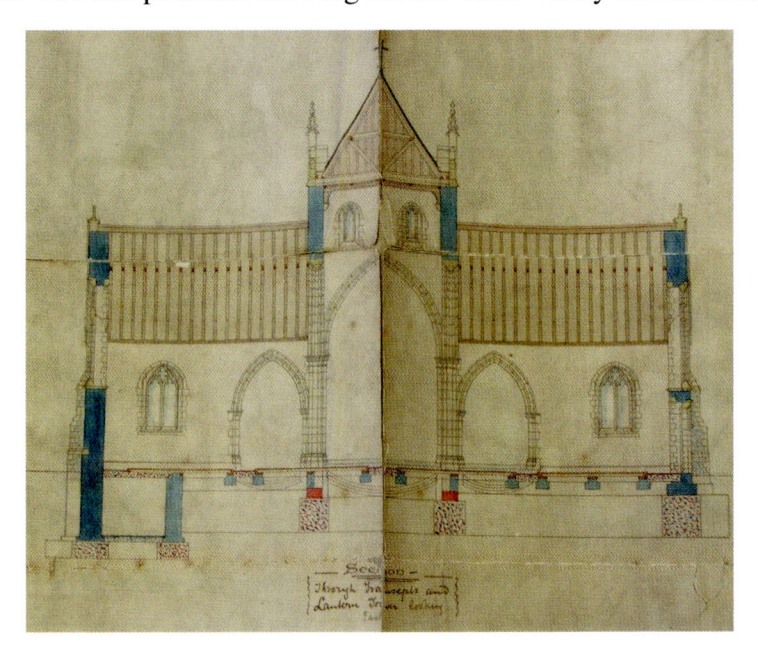

4.4 Cross section through enlarged church; note the supports under the North transept where some of the vaults lay and the inverse arches in the foundations designed to cope with movement in the clay on which the church is built. The inverse arch was something that Bingham was insistent on.

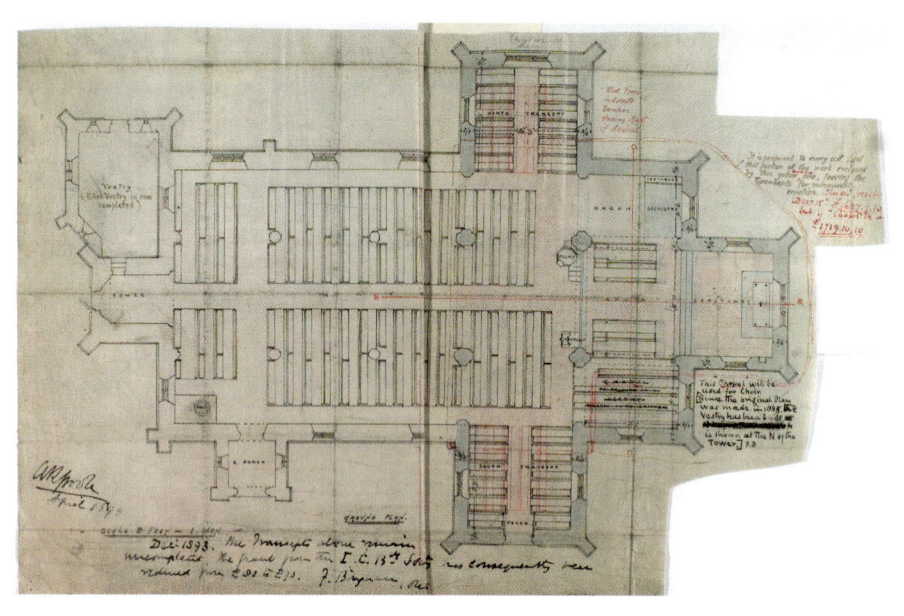

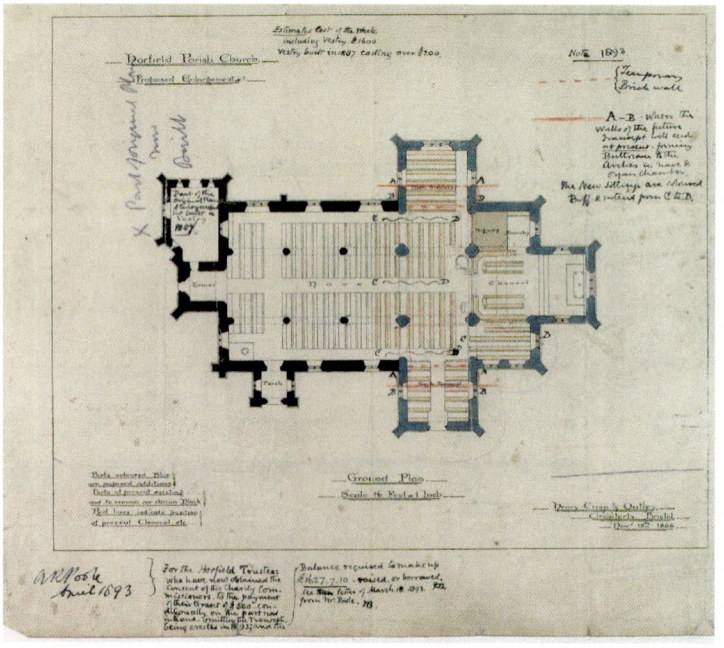

4.5  Detailed ground-plans showing what was planned and what was actually to be built in 1893.

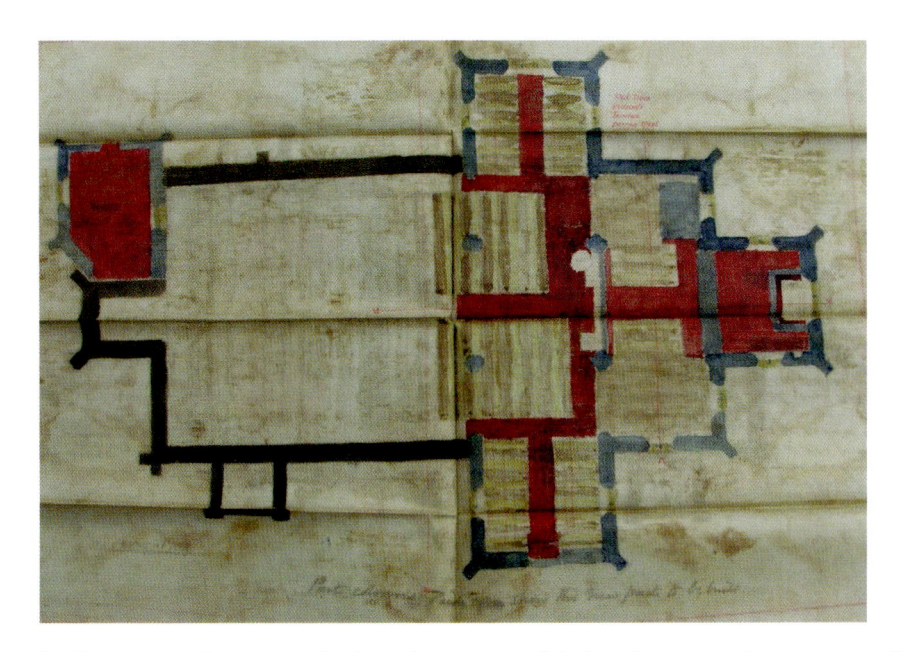

4.6   Reverse of a ground-plan drawn on fabric showing the extent of the work planned in c 1890. The plan also shows the choir vestry that had already been built. The South transept would not be completed until c1920 and the North transept until 1929.

4.7   South side of the church c1911 showing the wall stubs of the unfinished South transept. In another post-card of about the same date a large pile of rubble may be seen in the churchyard beside the path.

4.8  Photograph c1910, showing the East end of the church after the 1893 enlargement. Note that the East wall of the chancel around the window is not decorated.

4.9  Slightly later photograph c1912; wooden chancel screen removed and replaced by a carved stone screen. Note the decoration of the walls of the chancel. Also new gas lamps installed c 1900[24]

4.10  Photograph c1922, after the South transept was complete and the side chapel extended. Note the the old wooden pulpit has been replaced with a carved stone one to match the chancel screen

48

## 5.     The Last Stages

The church still lacked space in spite of all the works to date. This is shown by a licence issued on 14th November 1905[39], granting that the East end of the Edmunds Trust National Boys School, entirely screened off with a curtain during services, be used for all church services, because the parish church is too small. The license stipulates that baptisms celebrated at the school must be registered in the register held at the church. The licence says it is temporary, but cleverly, it did not have a closing date.

The last stages of the enlargement planned by Bingham were to take another thirty years and the reasons for this appear to have been wholly financial. In 1911 Messrs W V & A R Gough were invited to draw up new plans for the North & South transepts, the extension of the side chapel, a baptistry in place of the choir vestry, on the North side of the tower, an equivalent (matching) extension to the South aisle, a new Sacristy on the North side of the chancel and a new Organ loft[34]. The Goughs worked prolifically in Bristol from the 1890s until the early 1930s. There are at least eight churches in Bristol that they are known to have worked on. Moreover W V Gough was also the architect responsible for the Cabot Tower and the Granary Building.  The plans also included two additional clerestories one to be put in each side of the roof at the West end of the nave (Fig 5.2). Also included was the removal of the wooden chancel screen, the lower part of which may have been part of the original medieval screen[24]. This had been repositioned at the entrance to the chancel after each of the previous enlargements. In the Horfield PCC archives it says that the chancel screen was complete until 1764, when the upper portion "was lost". The screen was to be replaced with a stone parapet or frieze, 3ft (0.9m) high, with a metal gate in the gap. A faculty was granted for this work[35].

It is not clear exactly when the building work was completed, post-cards clearly show that some of the work was completed by c 1912 or 1913. Other post-cards suggest that the South transept may not have been completed until c1920 and even then not all the work was completed. The parts of the plans that were completed were the completion of the South Transept, to the new design and the extension of the side Chapel. Gough's design for the South transept differed from Crisp & Oatley's design because instead of a door on the South wall of the transept, the transept was to be entered via a porch on the East wall of the transept. The completion of the plan, the building of the North transept, would not take place for nearly a decade.

5.1 Church in early 1920s after the South transept had been completed.

5.2 Drawings by the Goughs that show how the church might look following their revision of Crisp and Oatley's plans for the transepts.

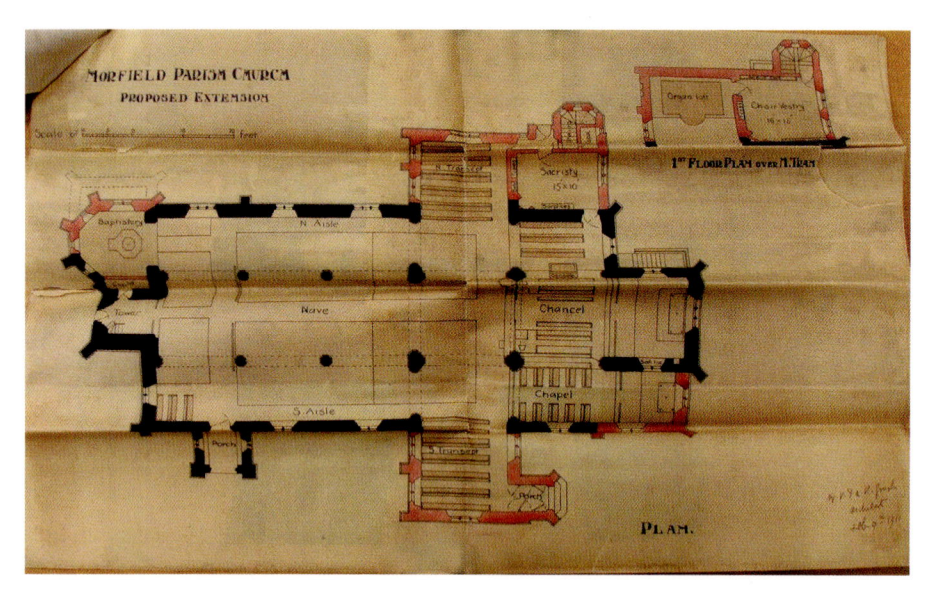

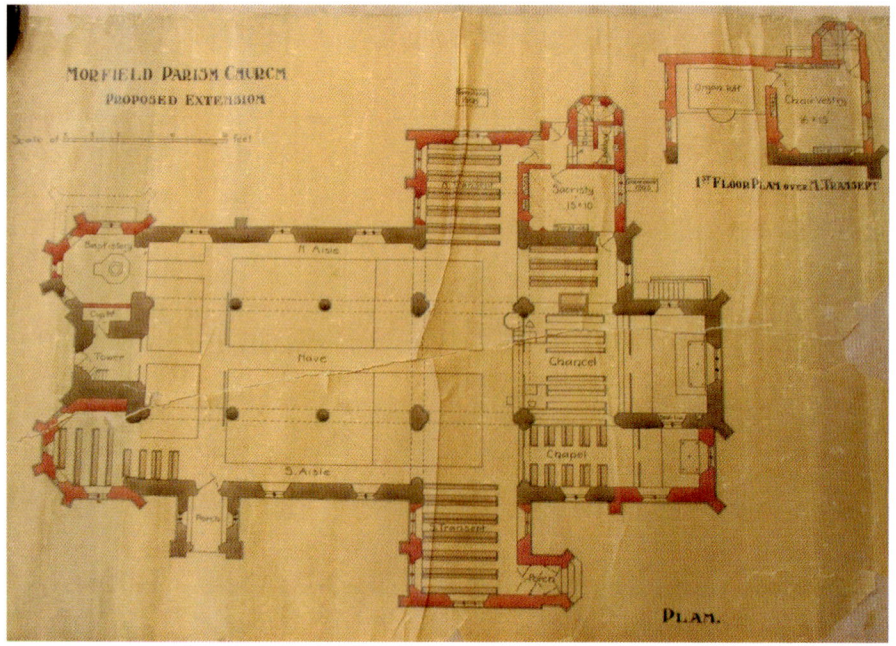

5.3 Two ground-plans drawn up by the Goughs that show their proposed changes to the plans of Crisp and Oatley; the extension to St Andrews chapel and the changes to the South transept were accepted.

Following the Great War of 1914-18, other commitments on the parish, including the enlargement of the St Edmunds Mission Church, formerly on Gloucester Road, and the building of a new church, St Gregory's in Upper Horfield meant that sufficient funds to complete the enlargement were not available until 1929. While no plans are known for the work that was carried out; there are a number of drawings, by Hartland-Thomas, diocesan surveyor, showing how it was intended the building should look inside and out[36] and there is the faculty[37], which lists the work that was to be carried out:

"To build a new North Transept with choir vestry, organ loft, engine house, lobby and WC attached. Clear out present organ chamber and rebuild organ in loft

To put an arch between the Sanctuary and the present chapel

To alter the levels in Sanctuary floor and to provide one step instead of two at the communion rail

To remove the platform and pews at the west end of the church and replace platform with block floor on concrete to match the rest

To provide chairs throughout

To rearrange electric light wires and fittings"

The last item supports a record in the Horfield PCC archive that electric lighting had been installed c1925-27. However, a document relating to building repairs probably carried out in the early 1930s, suggests that it may be a little later. The document though undated, refers to both the old and new transepts so must be post 1929, which suggests that there may still have been some gas lighting[40]. This document also refers to extensive repairs being needed to stonework and roofs. It mentions the tower, the belfry and drainage, including a drain that went under the North transept. It is also probable that the aumbry in the chapel was installed at this time or at least before the dedication service.

The work was carried out during the period when Henry S S Clarke was Rector. It was begun at the end of June 1929; on the 29th September it was closed for three weeks and during this time services were held at St Edmunds, under a licence granted on the 5th October 1929[38], which included allowing banns to be published and weddings solemnised. The church was reopened on 20th October 1929, the work finally completed early in 1930 and the church dedicated by the Bishop of Bristol on 25th February 1930. Fanshawe Bingham had hoped to be able to come to this service to see his dream completed, but he was prevented through illness.

As already mentioned, shortly after the completion of the work in 1929, extensive 'repairs' were needed and in 1944 further repair work had to be carried out. This later work was of such an extent that the church was out of use for several weeks. As a consequence a licence was issued to use the church hall for services during this time[41]. Details of the work carried out are not known. Consequently it is not possible to say if the work was needed as a result of problems with the quality of any of the work since the end of the 19th century, or was on the nave and nave roof, which by now were over one hundred years old.

The preceding chapters have only described the major phases of building that occurred during the 19th and 20th centuries. Other building works were carried out; notably the installation of the war memorials after each of the world wars and the installation of a new East window in 1909, in commemoration of the life of Adelaide Hutchinson, wife of the then rector of Horfield, Clement Hutchinson; Adelaide died at the rectory in 1908.

5.4 Architects drawings of the North Transept, also shown in the lower drawing are other buildings on the East side of the North transept.

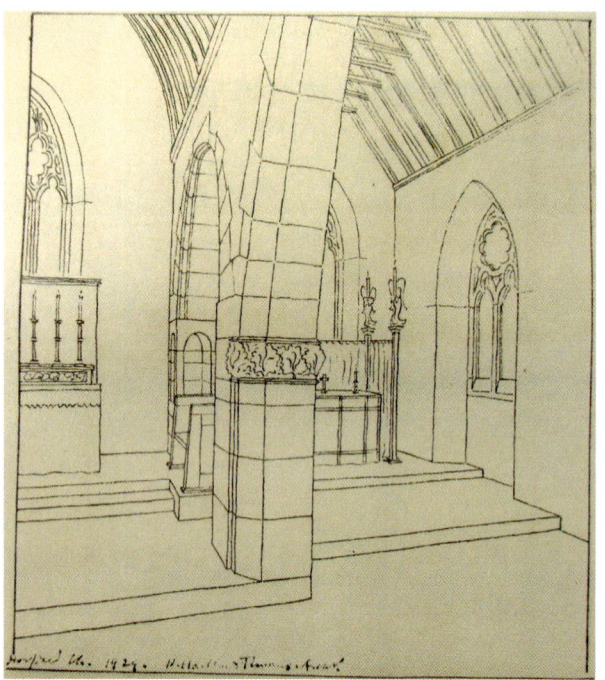

5.5 Architects drawing showing the arch, in place of a solid wall, between the chancel and the side altar; the piscina cut into the eastern end of the arch may also be seen.

5.6 Photograph c1937, showing the modifications to the chancel and side chapel carried out in 1929.

## 6. The Memorials within the Church

In 1750 Ralph Bigland a herald of the College of Arms began collecting information with the intention of producing a new history of the county of Gloucestershire. To this end, he and his helpers copied arms and made transcriptions from monuments across the county; many of these monuments have since disappeared or are now illegible. A review of his recorded inscriptions[43,] against those still surviving would suggest that Bigland surveyed Horfield before 1787 between two phases of inscription on the Pye memorial.

All of the petitions from the first in 1836 to those covering later building works, take great pains to make it clear that all marble and similar memorials in the church will be carefully removed, protected, and then replaced as close as is practicable within the church to their original location. That the church was successful in these endeavours may be shown by the fact that Bigland records four marble monuments and says that these were all in the chancel. Of the four marble monuments recorded by Bigland three still survive intact. The fourth monument to John Shadwell, has been replaced by a later monument that includes both John Shadwell and his wife Isabella; it is not known if there was insufficient space to add Isabella to the original memorial, or if it got damaged and so was replaced. Regardless of why the memorial was replaced, on the later memorial his age at death is given as 45, whereas on the earlier memorial it is given as 42. This is also the age given by Seyer in his note book and in the parish register[45]. As they protected earlier memorials on the walls so they equally protected later memorials and there is a good collection of memorials from the first half of the 19th century.

While marble wall memorials might have been protected, the same cannot be said for flat stones in the floor of the chancel; Bigland records eight in total including several early 17th century tombstones for the Walter family. Unfortunately none of these has survived. Bigland did not find/record a memorial for the first member of the family to be buried in Horfield, John Walter who was buried in

Horfield in 1502. In addition to the flat stones recorded by Bigland within the church, it is also probable that there was access to some of the burial vaults that would have been below the chancel. Some of these are known to have been very large. Bingham[44], in one of his letters, records that the Pye vault was 10 ft. (3.05m) square and about 8 or 9 ft. (c2.6) high. He says that the West arch of the central tower, facing the nave, was built over the Pye vault. It was filled with concrete to ensure the stability of the church He reports in a letter that "One of the foremen, when the concrete was pounded down over the solitary coffin, turned to me & said "He will find it hard to get out of that at the Resurrection"! "That thou sowest, thou sowest not that body that shall be" etc was all one could reply. In another letter Bingham records that the Shadwell vault was still extant with room left in it, after the work in 1893 had been completed. He says that when the North transept was built it would have been against the West wall. He says that when the 'stub' of the West wall for the North transept was built in 1893, it was made secure against any collapse of the sides of the vault. He also says that there were no graves in the part of the vault over which the North transept would be built. In the parish registers, Henry Richards notes that the Shadwell vault is under the vestry and opens on the outside. At the time of the burial of John Shadwell in July 1849, he says there was space for three more coffins. Today, immediately West of the West wall of the North transept is the family grave of John Mitchell Eugene Taylor Shadwell.

Most of the early memorials are on the wall above the door to the vestry behind the organ, where they have remained since 1893. Other mid 19th century and later memorials are spread around the church. These include two war memorials to those who gave their lives in the 1914-18 and 1939-45 wars.

Below are photographs and records of the inscriptions on the 18th and 19th century memorials in the church and the war memorials to those who died in the First and Second World Wars.

## On the East wall of the side chapel

To the Glory of God
In memory of "The Boy Hero" Archibald Walters
who gave his life to save his friend, Oct: 23$^{rd}$ 1874

## On the West Wall of the Nave

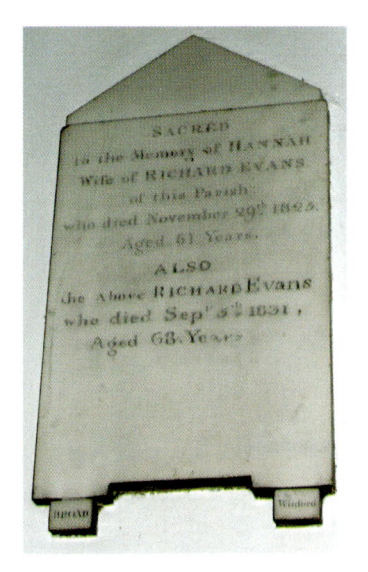

**Above**
To the memory of M$^{rs}$. Elizabeth Foot
Wife of the Rev$^d$. John Strode Foot
of Torr in the County of Devon
who died at Clifton Dec$^r$. 11$^{th}$. 1807
Aged 43 Years

**Left**  Sacred
to the memory of Hannah
wife of Richard Evans
of this parish
who died November 29$^{th}$. 1825.
Aged 61 years.
Also
the above Richard Evans
who died Sep$^r$ 5$^{th}$, 1831,
Aged 68 years

59

On the North wall of the nave.

To the memory of
John Frith Esq[r].
of Inniskillen Captain 72$^{nd}$ Highlanders
who died
at Horfield Barracks,
1$^{st}$ December 1850
aged 47 years.

In memory of
Charlotte Marmont
of Oakfield near Worcester,
whose remains are deposited in the chancel
of this Church,
she died at Clifton April 20$^{th}$. 1836,
aged 40.

In memory
of Isabella Daughter of
John Shadwell of the City of Cork Esq.
Lord of this Manor
she died the 3$^{rd}$. of July 1763
Aged 3 years & 2 months.

Her mother Isabella was Daughter of
Thomas Mitchell Esq[r].
late Lord of Said Manor
to whose Ancestors it hath belonged
for a long Series of Years.

60

On the South wall of the nave

Here rest the remains
of John Shadwell, Esq[r].
Barrister of the Inner Temple,
and Lord of this Manor,
who died at Brussels the 18th. April, 1777,
Aged 45.
He was descended from antient (*sic*) family
of the same name in Staffordshire,
and possessed highly cultivated talents
with a most benevolent heart.
ALSO
the remains of his beloved Wife Isabella,
who died in Bristol the 18th of May, 1815
in her 86th. Year:
having borne him nine children.
She was the third daughter of Thomas Mitchell, Esq[r].
late of Aghadda and Mitchell's Fort
in the County of Cork,
whose ancestor was companion with the Earl of Strigul
in the conquest of Ireland in the reign of Henry the II[d]
and among the first English settlers of distinction
in that Country.

―――――――――

At the top of the memorial are the arms of Shadwell : Per pale or, and az; on a chevron between three annulets, four escallops, all countercharged.

Esther Shadwell
Wife of John Shadwell. Esq$^r$. M.D.
died 22$^d$. January, 1818.
Aged 37.

*The mournful relics of a Wife most dear,*
*Of matchless excellence, lie buried here.*
*Long tried, but, not subdu'd by lingering pain,*
*Which art attempted to relieve in vain,*
*At length triumphant, her exulting soul*
*Has gain'd disastrous Life's immortal goal.*

Also to the memory of the above named John Shadwell M.D. who died at Southampton on the 6$^{th}$. day of July, 1849, Aged 87.

He was Lord Farmer of this Manor for 66 Years, it having been held by his family from the time of Henry VIII to his decease, when it passed into the hands of the Bishop of Gloucester and Bristol.

North wall of Organ Lobby

The majority of these monuments are from the 18th century or early 19th century and would have been present in the church before the first enlargement in 1836.

They are in four columns West to East.

The arrangement of the memorials is as follows:

Elisabeth Ridding

| Henry Savage | Elis. Jones | Mary Stock | Hester (Pye) |
| George Armstrong | Richard Jennings | Pye (family) | Lt. Col. Swyny |

This curious memorial which appears to be inscribed on a curved copper sheet is written in Latin and is a memorial to Elisabeth Anne Ridding. In situ it is almost illegible.

| | |
|---|---|
| IN MEMORIAM | In memory |
| ELISABETHE ANNE RIDDING | Elisabeth Anne Ridding |
| FIL NATU MAX THOMÆ RIDDING | Eldest daughter of Thomas Ridding |
| OLIM DE SOUTHAMPTON ARMIGERI | Formerly of Southampton Esquire |
| OBIT XVII DIE MAII A.S. MDCCCXLVII | Died 17th May, 1847 |
| ANNO ÆT.XVII | Aged 17 |

Elisabeth Ridding is buried at Walcot, Bath. She was buried May 23rd 1847. Elisabeth a cousin of Bishop Ridding of Southwell, died at Clifton while visiting Richards who was living there at the time[13].

Near this place lies interred
the body of Henry,
son of John and Rachel Savage, of Henleaze
he died the 24th August 1819,
Aged 3 years.
"Suffer little children to come unto me"

George Armstrong's memorial, left and gravestone, right.

The memorial reads

> To the memory of George Armstrong, Esq. born at Ballylin in the K.$^s$ C. Ireland, who after
> enduring the climate of Jamaica from A.D.1765 to 1791
> being at Bristol & a stranger lost his life by an opening left near
> the Drawbridge thro which he fell on the Night of the 18. Nov$^r$. 1799
> Aged 54 Y$^{rs}$.
> A Man of mild & modest manners, whose upright conduct thro life gain'd
> him many friends, but he never lost one, never missed the opportunity
> of doing a good action, or ever done a bad one.
> The kindest Husband and the fondest Father.
> This inscription is placed here by his unfortunate Widow & Chi [ldren]
> whose only consolation is the perfect knowledge that he always
> lived a life prepared for Dying.

His grave stone, which was found buried under turf on the north side of the church reads

> In memory of
> George Armstrong Esq
> who lost his life by Accident at Bristol
> Nov$^r$ 18$^{th}$ 1799.     Aged 54

Bingham says Armstrong's grave was discovered when the foundations for the South side of the chancel were being dug in 1893[13].

Also the remains of her niece
Eliz. Mary Ann Jones Spinster
Only child of the Rev$^d$ John Price Jones
late Rector of North Walsham Norfolk deceased
and Esther his wife afterwards Esther Shadwell.
She lived beloved
and died lamented
on the 5$^{th}$. Dec$^r$. 1812 in the 31$^{st}$ year of her age.

From
An experienced Sense
Of the many amiable Qualities
Which in every relation formed the Character
of
Richard Jennings Esq:
Late of this Parish
(whose remains lie here interred)
And to perpetuate their Memory,
His gratefull(*sic*) Widow
Rachel Jennings
Caused this stone to be erected.
He died the 9$^{th}$. of March, 1776
In the 54$^{th}$ year of his age

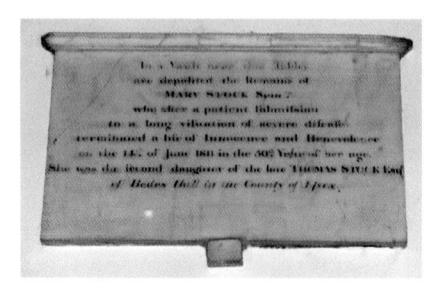

In a Vault near this Tablet
are deposited the remains of
Mary Stock, Spin$^{tr}$,
who after a patient submission
to a long visitation of severe disease
terminated a life of Innocence and Benevolence
on the 14$^{th}$. of June, 1811 in the 50$^{th}$. year of her age.
She was the second daughter of the late Thomas Stock, Esq,
of Bedes Hall in the County of Essex

In a Vault near this place
lie interr'd the remains of Hester Pye,
the loving and beloved wife of Samuel Pye,
of Bristol, Surgeon.
This Monument was erected by her afflicted
Husband, as the last Testimony of his unfeigned
affection for a truly virtuous Wife, a fond Parent,
and sincere Friend.
She departed this life January 15th. 1780
Aged 50.

Also of three of their Children,
Samuel, Frances, and Sophia
who died in their Infancy.

Also of Margaret Pye,
Mother of Samuel Pye who died 21st. April 1771,
Aged 80.
Also Mary Pye, Second Wife of Sam.l Pye,
died Dec.r 17th. 1787, Aged 60.
Also Eliz.h. Second Daughter of Sam.l Pye,
died Nov. 17th. 1790, Aged 23.
Also Sam.l. Pye died 24th Oct.r. 1809, Aged 80.
A truly Honest Man.

---

Hester Pye, Eldest and last surviving daughter
of the above Samuel Pye of Clifton, Esq.r
died 31st. August 1852 in the 86th. year of her age

Sacred
To the memory of
Hester,
(daughter of the late Thomas Pye, surgeon,
Clifton)
who departed this life March 6$^{th}$. 1881,
Aged 84 years.
"Willing to be absent from the body
and to be present with the Lord"
II COR. V.

Sacred to the memory of Lieutenant Colonel
Exham Schomburg Turner Swyny, 63$^{rd}$,, Reg$^t$,,
(eldest son of M$^{rs}$. Henry Shadwell by a former marriage
with Cap$^{tn}$,, Swyny, 60$^{th}$,, Rifles) who fell gallantly charging
the Russians at the Battle of Inkerman, Nov$^r$,,5$^{th}$,, 1854
and lies buried on Cathcarts Hill, deeply and deservedly
mourned by his Relatives and Friends as well, as by
his Brother Officers and all who knew him.
This Tablet was erected by his bereaved Widow and Relatives
as a slight Tribute of his worth and their affection and in the
firm hope that he who rests with the brave will also rise with the just.
"The trumpet shall sound and the dead shall be raised."

68

## Brass memorial plaques in window sills

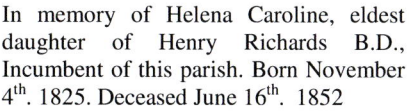

In memory of Helena Caroline, eldest daughter of Henry Richards B.D., Incumbent of this parish. Born November 4th. 1825. Deceased June 16th. 1852
"Blessed are the dead that die in the Lord, even so saith the spirit, for they rest from their labours".
14 Ch. Revelations 13 Verse

This is in the sill of the centre window in the North wall of the North aisle.

In memory of Mary Elizabeth, only surviving daughter of Henry Richards, Incumbent of this parish. Born 3rd. October 1834. Deceased 7th. September 1854.
"He is able to present you faultless before the presence of his glory with exceeding joy". Jude 24.

This is next to the plaque shown above in the same sill.

To the glory of God and in affectionate remembrance of Edward George, 3rd son of Robert Montague and Frances Vining Worlock who died in Adelaide, May 19th. 1881. Aged 24 years. R.I.P.

This is in the sill of the western most window in the South wall of the South aisle.

Windows

These two glass quarries are in the lower part of the eastern of the two windows in the South aisle.

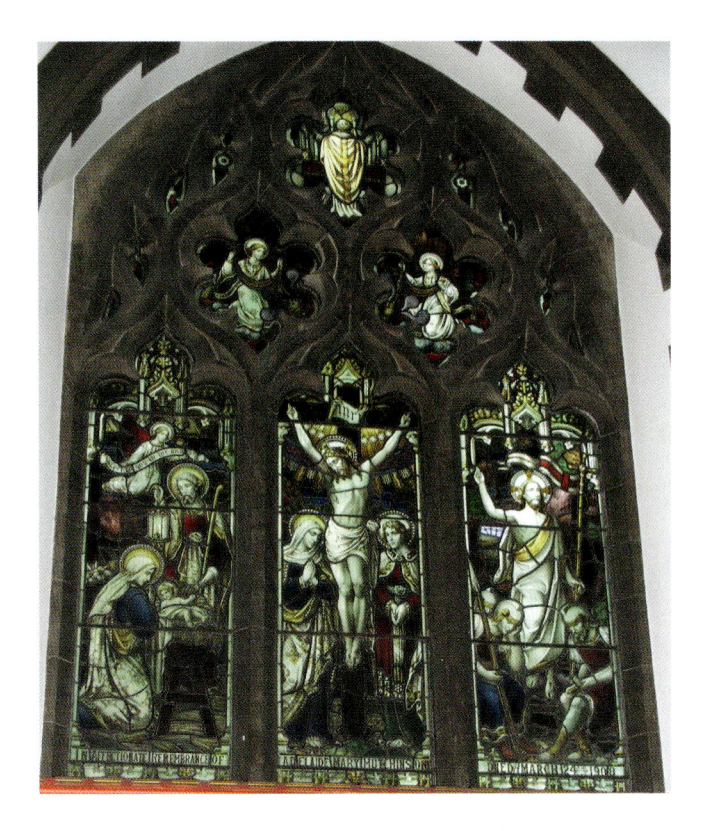

The East window of the church a memorial to Adelaide Mary Hutchinson; the inscription across the bottom of the three lights reads

In affectionate remembrance of   Adelaide Mary Hutchinson   Died March 24$^{th}$ 1908

Below the piscina that is carved into the arch that separates the main alter from the side chapel is a brass plate that reads

A.M.D.G.
AND IN MEMORY OF
ADELAIDE MARY HUTCHINSON,
WHO DIED MARCH 24$^{TH}$ 1908.
AT HORFIELD RECTORY,
THE STAINED GLASS IN THE EAST WINDOW
OF THIS CHURCH IS PLACED HERE BY HER HUSBAND
THE REV. CLEMENT HUTCHINSON,
RECTOR OF THIS PARISH
REQUIESCAT IN PACE

# First World War Memorial in South Transept

To the Glory of God
and in the memory of our brothers
who fell in the Great War 1914-1919.
This crucifix was placed here by
some of those for whom they died.
Jesu Mercy.

| | | |
|---|---|---|
| Appleby, A. | Harding, G.H. | Richardson, E. |
| Appleby , B. | Headford, W. | Robbins, G. A. |
| Baker, V. | Heginbottom, E. | Robinson, D.B. |
| Beaman , H. E. | Hill, W.A. | RoIes,R,H. |
| Bennett, H. J. | Jenkinson, H. | Savage, S.G.V. |
| Brooks, B. | Jennings, A. T. | Scaife G.E. |
| Burrows, H. H. | Jones, W. A. | Scull,F. |
| Burrows, J. | Knight,W. | Scull ,H.W. |
| Clark, C. | Lewis , L. | Slade,E.M. |
| Clark, P. | Mackie,D.J. | Stait, G.J. |
| Coggins, R. L. | Marden, S, | Stamp, F.A. |
| Coles, F. | Midwinter, H. | Symington, H.G. |
| Cordwell, F. | Mitchell ,W. | Thomas, J. |
| Durbin, W. H. | Murray, E.W. | Thomson, D. |
| Exel1, J. | North, H. S. M, | Weeks, R.A. |
| Feaver, S.D. | Palmer, R. | Whitman, R. |
| Fry, A. C. | Pierce, F. | Wilkins, M. |
| Fry, E. E. | Press, T.C. | Williams, H.L. |
| Gidley, H. | Puttick , F. | Willis, H. |
| Gordon, F.A. | Rew, J. | Woollen, J. |
| Gould, C.G. | | Yates, E |

# Second World War Memorial Window in South Transept

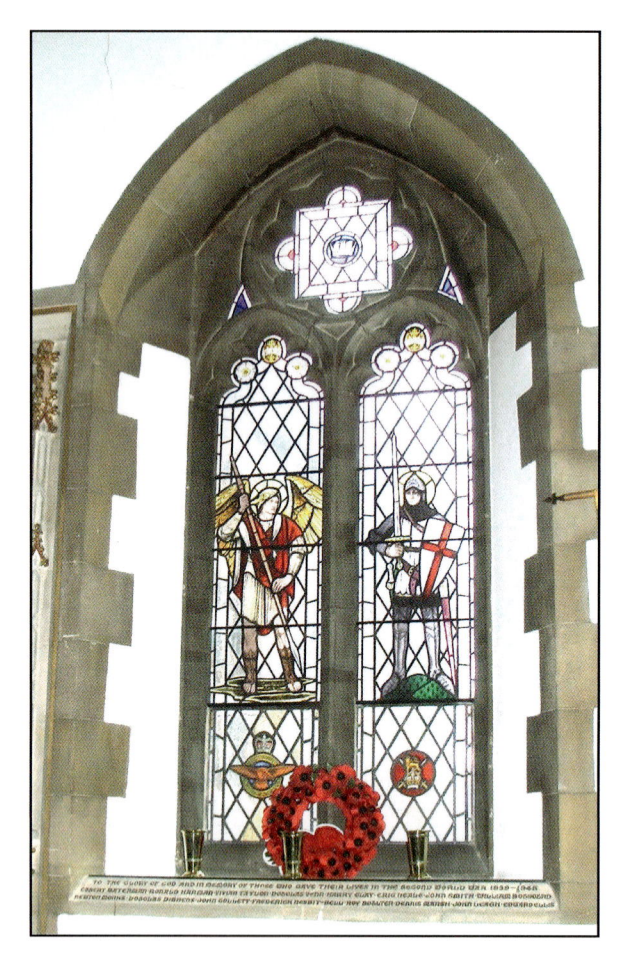

To the glory of God and in memory of those who gave their lives in the Second World War 1939-1945

Egbert Waterman. Ronald Harman. Vivian Taylor. Douglas Venn. Harry Clay. Eric Neale. John Smith. William Bougourd. Newton Monks. Douglas Dibbens. John Collett. Frederick Nesbit-Bell. Roy Boulter. Dennis Marsh. John Leagh. Edward Ellis

## 7. Memorials in the Churchyard

The churchyard was approximately circular until the mid 19th century, when some land was added, on the South East side and possibly some was removed when the school was built, it covers an area of 1.23 acres (0.47 hectares). When people were first buried in the churchyard is not known. The earliest burial registers date from 1543[45]. In 1946 the graveyard was surveyed and a total of 1338 grave plots were identified, but most of them were not identifiable to an individual or family.

If graves as opposed to memorials inside the church, survived poorly, the situation in the churchyard is even worse. None of the 18th century tombs recorded by Bigland has survived and of the twenty one graves, head and flat-stones, recorded by Bigland, five have survived. Two are legible and identifiable (those to Thomas Latcham and his wife, Elizabeth), two have some inscription remaining and have been tentatively identified as the graves of Mary Taylor and either Mary or Hannah Organ and one has no surviving inscription. All the surviving graves are close to the south porch. There are a number of reasons for the poor level of survival. The increase in the size of the church would have meant that graves close to the church, particularly on the South side, usually the preferred side in a graveyard, would have had to be moved and during this operation tombstones could have been damaged. The drawing of the church as it stood before the 1836 rebuilding work shows several graves up against the East wall of the chancel. Clearly at some point in the 19th century, probably about the time that the 1893 work was carried out, there was a clearance or removal of late 18th and early 19th century gravestones, which were then used for paving around the East end of the church and a path to the North East side of the church. Similarly the building of the South transept resulted in the removal of several graves, including a tomb surrounded by iron railings, which is visible on many later 19th and early 20th century pictures. It is possible that it was older. The earliest known picture of the church shows very few graves in the graveyard and several mid 18th century graves that are still extant are not shown; the artist seems mainly concerned with the church. A faculty is needed for the removal of any gravestone or tomb, but with the exception of the faculties associated with the various major building phases in the 19th and early 20th centuries, no others have been found besides that granted in 1967[46]. The 1967 faculty, which gave approval to level soil mounds on all graves not "now tended and cared for" and the removal of ten headstones and six kerbs on the South side of the church in order that broad grass paths might be cut through to the boundary hedge and other areas cleared for mowing, help to explain why stones have gone missing. Some memorials have been lost through erosion and a walk around the churchyard gives a good indication of what and what not to have a gravestone carved from if you want it to survive for centuries. Some early 19th century memorials are more legible than others carved much later. A few memorials remain but have lost their legibility not through erosion, but because of fashion, in this case the use of lead lettering that was 'pinned' to the stone. Over time the letters disappear, just leaving the holes to show where they were. A brief survey of the graveyard was carried out by some members of the Bishopston, Horfield and Ashley Down Local History Society in 2007 to assess how many of the graves recorded by Bigland were still present; but there is a need for a formal study to record all the surviving graves.

The 2007 survey gave further evidence to show that Horfield was not just a burial ground for people from Horfield or Filton, but was also a place where people who lived in Bristol or were visiting Bristol, might be buried, particularly in the late 18th and early 19th centuries. Besides various people from Bristol, including the Pye family who had a huge vault, there are burials recorded for people from Worcester, Norfolk, Devon and Essex, either in the church or in the graveyard. Most of the people were probably wealthy and several died while visiting Clifton. At least one of these was visiting Clifton when the hot wells were still in use, ie before 1822. Among the notable non-Horfield people whose graves have so far been identified are William Pether, the noted engraver and painter; Captain Benjamin Runwa RN, who was a naval captain of the line in the 18th century and was one of the sponsors of a book about North America that was published shortly after American independence, and John Frost, the famous chartist leader; who after being sentenced to death for treason, had his sentence commuted and he was transported for life to Australia. Following a campaign, he was eventually allowed to return to England and he lived out the remainder of his days in Stapleton.

As to why some of these and others whose tombstones have yet to be transcribed were buried in Horfield is not clear but it is very probable that the reason was linked to restrictions on burials within the city, where many graveyards were very full by the 19th century, and to burial fees. Burial fees were a source of income to clergy and in London and other parts of the country it has been recorded that poor clergy made a significant part of their annual income through burial fees. In some parishes the money was split between the clergy and the parish, which increased the incentive to secure bodies for burial. Horfield was always a poor parish and there is correspondence from William Moseley, who was curate of Horfield in 1708, and later clergy in Horfield, complaining about how poor the parish was and how little money the clergy received. It is highly probable that Horfield clergy from the late 18th century until the middle of the 19th century let it be known, within Bristol and Clifton that they would be prepared to bury people from outside their parish. In London the fees for vaults were even higher than fees for burial in the church yard and again it is likely that this was an option that was offered; most of the memorials within the church related to people who were buried in the church, ie in vaults, not in the church yard.

There are numerous military graves in the graveyard, including a number of Commonwealth War Graves Commission graves, mostly linked to the First World War. Some of the others are clearly linked to the barracks, which while having its own chapel, did not have its own graveyard. In other cases it is assumed that the individual commemorated, particularly where the memorial is from fellow serving soldiers, had some link to Horfield. Many of these are becoming difficult to read, including at least one of the War Graves

Commission graves and ought to be recorded. It is clear from some of the descriptions that there are some lives worthy of investigation.

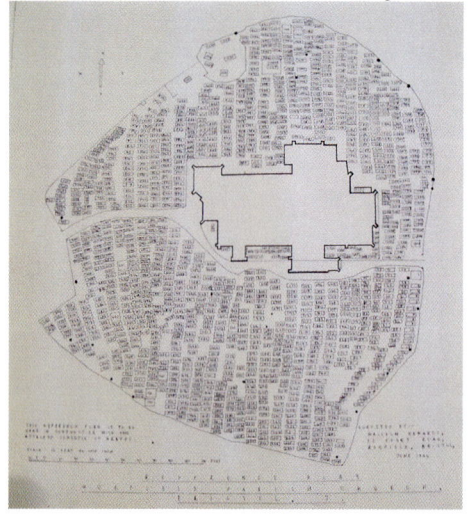

Plan of graveyard drawn up in 1946 showing all known, but not necessarily identified graves.

Below are photographs of some the older and/or more unusual gravestones. The graveyard has not been properly surveyed, with regards to recording the design of the memorials and the inscriptions and it is probable that there are other gravestones of interest, with a story to tell.

Part of the graveyard near the South porch. The gravestones in the foreground are the oldest identified graves in the graveyard. No surviving inscription has been found on the near left hand stone.

These two head stones of similar design are the oldest known surviving monuments, with inscriptions, in the graveyard, indeed in the whole church. The left-hand stone has no legible name but seems to be dated June 1716 and probably marks the grave of Mary Taylor. The right-hand stone also marks the grave of a woman possibly Mary or Hannah Organ. There is no legible name or date, only a fragment of a dedication, most of which is underground, where it has been very well preserved.

In Mem[orium]
……………………
………… ………….who
died June ye…...…
…1716……………
…..27 y[ears]……..

Born……..……
first………no…
….mo…………
……..…………
world…………
*the world her
worth thus
phenix like as she
was born to bless*

79

## A pair of head stones for Thomas Latcham.

The west-facing inscription reads

In Memory of
Thomas Latcham of ye Parish
Of Filton Yeoman who died A[ug]
Aged 85

The east-facing inscription consists of a fine home-spun verse, roundly telling malicious gossips to look to their own households

TL 1749
Farewel vain world I've seen enough of thee
And now am careless what thou say'st of me
Thy smiles I court not nor thy frowns I fear
My cares are past my Head lies quiet here
What faults thou saw'st in me take care o [n?]
And look at Home enough there's to be do[ne?]
Farewell dear Wife & Children all
For all must go when Christ do call

In Memory
of Elizabeth Relict of
Thomas Latcham of the
Parish of Filton Yeoman: who died
Sep$^{br}$:y$^e$ 19$^{th}$: 1757 Aged 82
Who after a teadious travail
Thro this vale of tears
Here sweetly sleeps
From life how happy in release
No more by woes oppressed
Troubling here the wicked cease
The weary are at rest

Here lieth the remains of
Maria Scudamore
Who died the 17th of May 1805,
late Wife of W.R.Scudamore Esq.

Sacred
To the memory of
Sarah Sweet Townley
only daughter of Wm & Louisa Townley.
(of the parish of Stapleton)
who departed this life
May 26th. 1837
Aged 12 years.
*Why do we mourn departing friends,*
*Or shake at deaths alarms*
*Tis but the voice that Jesus sends*
*To call them to his arms*

Sacred
To the memory of
Benjamin Runwa
Master and Commander of the
Royal Navy who departed this
life at Bristol the 8th of July 1807
Aged 72.

*In him was united the Polite*
*Gentleman Indulgent Landlord*
*Kind Master & Sincere Friend. He*
*lived beloved & died regretted by*
*all who had the Pleasure*
*of his Acquaintance.*

It is possible that this stone which now lies between the porch on the South transept and the South wall of the side chapel may not be in its exact original position. It would have been difficult to build around this and an adjacent grave. Bingham says that the upper part of the coffin was sawn off and the skull placed further in the coffin[13].

John Frost
1784 – 1877
Mayor of Newport 1836
Chartist Leader 1839
Mary Frost
1782 – 1857
Henry Hunt Frost
1822 – 1842
*The outward mark of respect*
*paid to men merely because*
*they are rich & powerful…..*
*hath no communication*
*with the heart*

This is a modern stone and it is not known if the inscription is an accurate copy of the inscription on the original stone.

Sacred to the memory of
William Pether
Who died July 19th 1821
Aged 82 years

He was an Artist of distinguished abilities

Also
Elizabeth Pether
who died June 19th 1833
Aged 84 years

Joseph Overbury's
Burial Ground
July 1825

Joseph Overbury married Hester Park of Stapleton at Horfield in June 1822. There is no record of his burial in Horfield. However, Edward Overbury of St Michael (aged 2 months) was buried in Horfield in July 1824

[H] ere
……….Remains of
[Josiah] Stevens Esq[r].
……..Parish, and of
[Kingst]on, Surry,
[departe]d this life on the
……….March 1822
[39] Year of his Age.

….[a]nd justly esteem[ed]
…, his loss is s………….
…l, or grieve ………..
……….ls a……….

Josiah "was a maltster in Kingston, and also occupied a farm near Bristol". After his death his executors and others were involved in a court case which has become part of English case law.

There are two of these curiously designed grave memorials in the graveyard, both are carved from sandstone and sadly both are quite badly decayed. A large piece has broken off the back of the Bligh memorial shown below, which Bingam describes as being in poor condition[13].

…………………………
…[d]eposited…………………
[W]illiam Blig[h]
..........d Son of
……….…….. Theodosi…
[departe]d this life
… [Cli]fton.
……..October 18….

Beneath this Monument
is deposited the body of
WILLIAM BLIGH, third Son of
Thomas and Lady Theodosia Bligh.
He departed this life at Clifton,
On the 24th October 1810,
In the 15th year of his age.

"Blessed are the pure of heart for they shall see God"     5 Ch.S.Matthew, v.8
"The Lord gave and the Lord hath taken away; Blessed be the Name of the Lord," 1 Ch. Job,v.21
Transcribed by Bingham[13]

83

The Richard's family plot on the North side of the graveyard. The railings have gone, one grave has been toppled off its base and the text on several of them is illegible because of weather damage. The plight of these memorials is typical of many within the graveyard.

Behind to the left, on the edge of the picture is the Latcham family memorial.

# 8. The Bells

There are five bells in the West tower, in what is said to be the smallest five bell tower in England; it is also reported to be the only five bell tower in the Bristol area. Until 1997 all the bells in the tower were of 18th century date, but following an accident, 1997, the 4th was replaced by a 19th century bell from Petherton in Somerset.

It is not known if the tower, which dates to the 15th century, had any bells before the late 17th century, but the design of the tower suggests that it was intended for bells. In other parts of the country it is known, or at least recorded that bells were removed from churches during the English Civil War and melted down. Horfield had bells by the early 18th century. Bishops transcripts report a cracked bell and a decaying bell loft in the 1730s, suggesting that the bells had been there for some considerable time.

Besides the inscriptions on the bells themselves and what can be deduced from that information nothing is known about who bought the bells and exactly when they were hung. Who financed the purchase of the bells would be of particular interest given the overall poverty of the population of the parish in the 18th century and the lack of care and finance for the up keep of the church, of which the parlous state of the fabric by the early part of the 19th century is testament. There are comments about the state of the bells and the bell loft in early 18th century Bishops' transcripts. This lack of information is mainly because there are few direct surviving records for the church; the registers are an exception, before the early part of the 19th century.

Details of the bells are as follows:

| Bell Identification | Note | Weight* | Diameter | Inscription** |
|---|---|---|---|---|
| Treble | F | 229 kg (4½ cwt) | 0.74m (29 inches) | I. Parker . C.Warden. 1807 John Rudhall Fect. |
| 2nd | E♭ | 216 kg (4¼ cwt) | 0.69m (27 inches) | Fear God & Honour the King A.B.F. 1773 |
| 3rd | D | 241 kg (4¾ cwt) | 0.79m (31 inches) | ABM.B.F. Thos. Francombe & Thos. Jenkins Hangers 1773 |
| Current 4th *** | C | - | - | Mears & Stainbank, Founders, London 1896 In Memory of Edward George Ruscombe Pool Born January 10th 1882 Died October 16th 1894 |
| Old 4th | C | 279 kg (5½ cwt) | 0.81m (32 inches) | Thomas Sweeting Church Warden. ABM Bilbie Fecit 1773 |
| Tenor | B♭ | 394kg (7¾ cwt) | 0.94m (37 inches) | George the IIId. King Defender of the Faith & Dr Newton Lord BP. of Bristol. A.B.F 1773 John Shadwell Esq. Lord of the Manor of Horfield |

\*        The weights shown are the weights of the bells in their original condition with canons. The canons were removed when the bells were re-hung in 1982. At that time the original wooden supporting beams of oak and elm were replaced by a new frame work of cast iron and steel. The current weight of the tenor is now given as 368kg (7¼ cwt)

\*\*       The inscriptions on the bells are described in several documents including Horfield Miscellanea[13] several documents in the Horfield PCC archive and in the bell tower itself. However the exact wording and the order of the wording differs between most of them. The information above is taken from the information in the bell tower.

\*\*\*      The current 4th bell came from South Petherton in Somerset; it replaced the old 4th bell in 1998, following the 'collapse' of the old bell during a bell ringing practice session 1997.

Thomas Sweeting who was named on the old 4th bell, was landlord of The Ship alehouse.

John Rudhall who cast the Treble was a bell founder in Gloucester. He was the last of a long dynasty of bell founders in Gloucester, dating back to the 17$^{th}$ century who eventually sold their business to the Whitechapel foundry in London in the early 19$^{th}$ century.

The Bilbie family of Chew stoke in Somerset likewise had a long history of bell founding and there are churches throughout the surrounding counties with bells from both foundries.

It is said that you need a minimum of five bells to ring a peal. This suggests that there was a treble bell before 1807 and that the treble bell was not new in 1807 but may have been re-cast, possibly from a treble originally manufactured by the Bilbie family. But it is equally possible that the treble was the last of an older set of bells to 'fail' and that the others had been re-cast in 1773. Unfortunately, unless new documents come to light either linked to Horfield parish church or either of the two bell foundries, we will never know the answer.

Views in the bell tower.

Part of the inscription on the tenor bell.

The full inscription reads

George the IIId. King Defender of the Faith & Dr Newton Lord BP. Of Bristol. A.B.F 1773 John Shadwell Esq. Lord of the Manor of Horfield

In the picture it is possible to clearly read ...ORFIELD on the third line and A B F on the line above.

## 9. The Clock

There are no obvious makers marks or similar either on the workings of the clock or the face but it is clearly visible on a post card that may be dated to c 1850. There was a clock, possibly the current clock, installed in the tower before the 1847 enlargement. Part of the justification in 1847 for removing the gallery seating in the tower was because of the danger to children from the clock weights.

Left:   Clock face in South face of tower

Below left: Clock mechanism

Below: Weights for clock

## 10. The Organ

**History**

Bingham[13] says there was a "very small" one manual organ in the church that had been installed in 1836. He says that it had been donated to the church by the Reverend Raymond Barker.

The current organ was originally built by Palmer of King Square, Bristol, in 1885, and has been added to over the years. In 1929 the organ was moved from the North chancel aisle to the new organ chamber in the North transept and at the same time a significant amount of modernisation was carried out. This included replacing the pneumatic action that had connected the detached consol to the organ by an electric action. During this work, which was carried out by W G Vowels Ltd of Bristol, a fine Tuba stop was removed. A further re-building took place in 1994 following receipt of a generous legacy, during which the Trumpet and other stops were added to the great organ, with further additions to the swell and pedal departments. This has resulted in a versatile instrument well suited to both the accompaniment of the church services and for recitals, and of which Horfield can be justly proud[48].

The organ console

The pipes for the organ are in the organ loft which is in the North transept

## Specification

Two manual and 32 note pedal board.
Electric action, manual swell pedal.
Pipes are housed in upper chamber.
Detached console situated to the side of the chancel, facing the choir.
Much of the pipe-work dates from the nineteenth/early twentieth century instrument.
Rebuilt in the early 1990's.

| Great | Swell | Pedal |
|---|---|---|
| Open Diapason 8' | Open Diapason 8' | Oboe 4' from swell |
| Clarabelle 8' | Salicional 8' | Oboe 8' from swell |
| Dulciana 8' | Lieblich Gedacht 8' | Oboe 16' from swell |
| Harmonic Flute 4' | Vox Celeste 8' | Twenty second 2' |
| Principal 4' | Principal 4' | Fifteenth 4' |
| Twelfth 22/3 | Chimney Flute 4' | Bass Flute 8' |
| Fifteenth 2' | Fifteenth 2' | Principal 8' |
| Tierce 13/5' | Larigot 11/3 | Bourdon 16' |
| Mixture 2 ranks | Mixture 2 ranks | Open Wood 16' |
| Trumpet 8' | Cornopean 8' | |
| | Oboe 8' | |
| | Contra Oboe 16' | **Couplers** |
| | **Couplers** | Swell to Pedal |
| | Swell Octave | Great to Pedal |
| | Swell to Great | |

The most recent rebuild was by A. W. Cawston of Dursley, Gloucestershire, who now cares for the organ. This involved some tonal modification and improvement of the action, including the addition of the Great Trumpet, Swell Chimney Flute, extension of the 16ft. Swell Contra Oboe to the pedal section and adjustments to the mixture stops[48].

It is reported that during the rebuild in 1994 it was discovered that the Rockingham Electric Blower was discovered to have been wired incorrectly and was rotating in the wrong direction[24].

# Appendix 1

## Proposed stages in the building of the early parish church at Horfield

Early to mid 12th century - small stone built chapel

Early to mid 13th century - chancel added and probably porch

15th century - tower added at West end of nave

# Appendix 2

## Development of Horfield Parish Church during the 19th and 20th Centuries

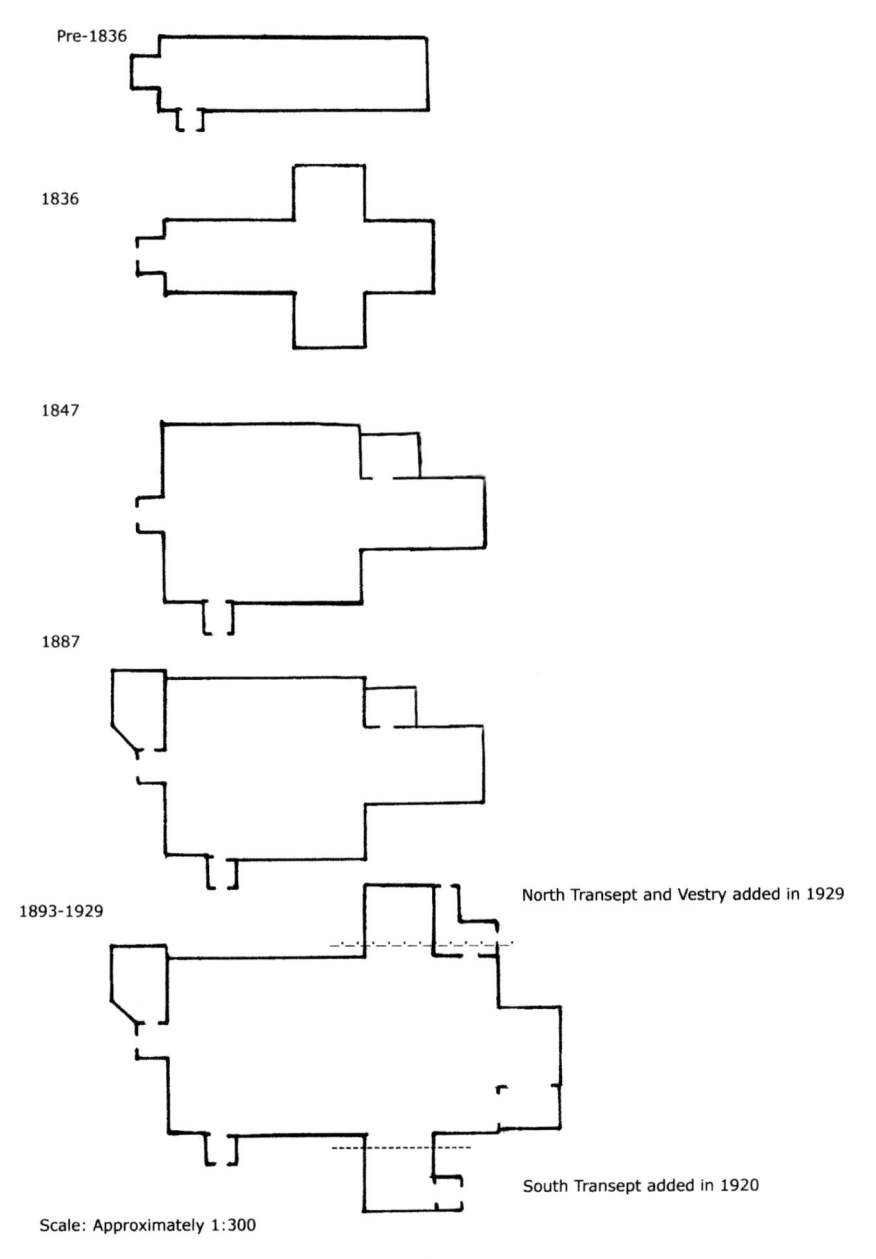

Pre-1836

1836

1847

1887

1893-1929

North Transept and Vestry added in 1929

South Transept added in 1920

Scale: Approximately 1:300

# Appendix 3

Photograph of the 1836 petition for a faculty for the first enlargement of the church.

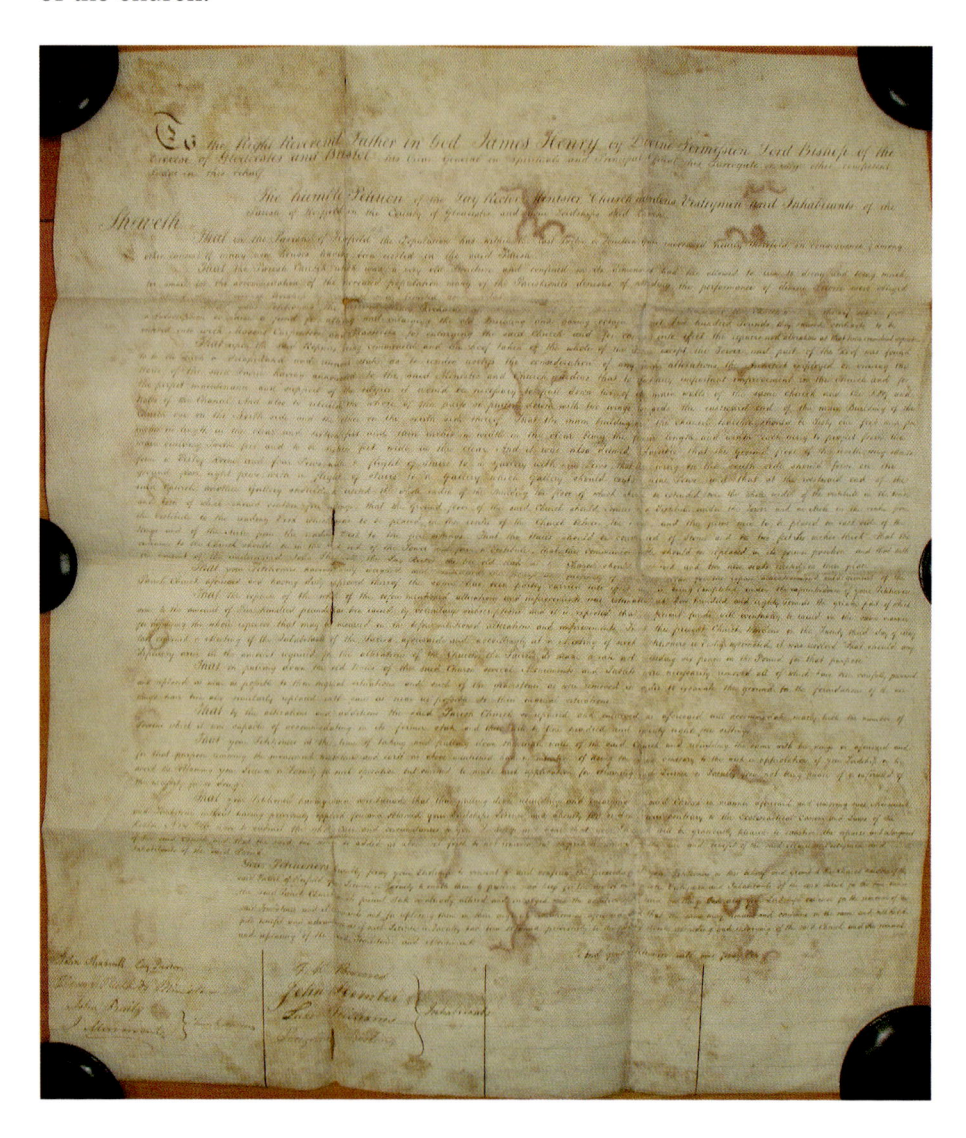

# Transcription of the 1836 petition for a faculty for the first enlargement of the church.

**To** the Right Revered Father in God James Henry by Divine permission Lord Bishop of the Diocese of Gloucester and Bristol his Vicar General and Principal Official his Surrogate or any other competent judge in this behalf.

The humble petition of the lay rector, minister, churchwardens vestrymen and inhabitants of the parish of Horfield in the county of Gloucester and your lordships said diocese.
**Sheweth**
That in the Parish of Horfield the population has within the last 12 or 14 years increased nearly threefold in consequence (among other causes,) of many new houses having been erected in the same Parish.

That the Parish Church which was a very old structure and confined in its dimensions had been allowed to run to decay, and being much too small for the accommodation of the increased population many of the Parishioners desirous of attending the performance of Divine Worship were obliged to attend other places of worship by reason of such limited accommodation.

That your Petitioners The Reverend Henry Richards the Minister and John Bailey and James Marmont the Church Wardens thereof set on foot a subscription to raise a fund for altering and enlarging the old building and having obtained about five hundred pounds they caused contracts to be entered into with Masons, Carpenters and Plasterers for enlarging the same Church and for carrying into effect the repairs and alterations at that time considered requisite.

That upon the said repairs being commenced and the roof taken off the whole of the fabric except the Tower and part of the roof was found to be in such a dilapidated and ruinous state as to render useless the consideration of any such alterations, the Architect employed on viewing the walls of the said fabric having announced to the said Minister and Church Wardens that to effect any important improvement in the Church and for the perfect maintenance and support of the edifice it would be necessary to pull down two of the main walls of the same Church and the roof and the walls of the Chancel and also rebuild the whole of the parts so pulled down with two wings towards the eastward end of the main Building of the Church one on the north side and the other on the south side thereof – That the main building and the Chancel together should be sixty one feet and five inches in length in the clear and sixteen feet and three inches in width in the clear being the former length and width, each wing to project from the main building twelve feet and to be sixteen feet wide in the clear. And it was also deemed advisable that the ground floor of the North wing should form a vestry room and four pews with a flight of stairs to a gallery with nine pews that the wing on the South side should form on the ground floor eight pews with a flight of stairs to a gallery which gallery should contain nine pews, and that at the Westward end of the said Church another gallery should be erected the whole width of the building the floor of which should be extended over the whole width of the vestibule in the Tower and both of which should contain free sittings.

That the ground floor of the said Church should consist of a vestibule under the Tower and an aisle in the centre from the vestibule to the Reading desk which was to be placed in the centre of the Church between the wings, and the pews were to be placed on each side of the wings and of the aisle from the Reading Desk to the free sittings. That the walls should be constructed of stone and be two feet thick six inches thick - that the entrance to the Church should be in the west end of the Tower and form a vestibule - that the Communion Table should be replaced its former position and that with the consent of the undersigned John Shadwell Lay Rector the two old seats in the Chancel should be removed and two new seats erected in their place.

That your Petitioners having duly weighed and considered the fitness and propriety of the above Plan for the repair alterations and enlargement of the Parish Church aforesaid and having duly approved thereof the same has been partly carried into effect and is being completed under the superintendence of your Petitioners.

That the expense of the whole of the before mentioned alterations and improvements was estimated at five hundred and eighty pounds the greater part of which sum to the amount of five hundred pounds has been raised by voluntary subscriptions and it is expected that sufficient funds will eventually be raised in the same manner, for defraying the whole expenses that may be incurred in the before mentioned alterations and improvements.

That the present Church Wardens on the twenty third day of May last convened a meeting of the Inhabitants of the Parish aforesaid and accordingly at a meeting of such petitioners in vestry assembled it was resolved "That should any deficiency arise in the amount required for the alteration of the Church, the Parish do make a rate not exceeding sixpence in the pound for that purpose".

That on pulling down the walls of the said Church several monuments and tablets were necessarily removed all of which have been carefully preserved and replaced as near as possible to their original situations, and such of the gravestones as were removed in order to excavate the ground for the foundations of the new wings have also been similarly replaced with care as near as possible to their original situations.

That by the alterations and additions to the said Parish Church so repaired and enlarged will accommodate nearly treble the number of persons which it was capable to accommodating in its former state and there will be one hundred and twenty eight free sittings.

That your petitioners at the time of taking and pulling down the main walls of the said Church and rebuilding the same with two wings as aforesaid and for that purpose removing the monuments, tombstones and earth as above mentioned had no intention of doing the same contrary to the wish or approbation of your Lordship or to avoid the obtaining your Licence or Faculty for such operation, but omitted to make such application for obtaining your License or Faculty from not being aware of or informed of the necessity for so doing.

That your Petitioners having since ascertained that their pulling down, rebuilding and enlarging the said Church in manner aforesaid and removing such monuments and tombstones without having previously applied for and obtained your Lordship's Licence and Faculty for so doing was contrary to the Ecclesiastical Canons and Laws of the Realm, Now beg leave to submit the whole case and circumstances to your Lordship and hope that your Lordship will be graciously pleased to sanction the repairs and enlargement of the said Church and that the said two wings so added as above set forth be not removed but suffered to remain for the use and benefit of the said Minister, Vestrymen and Inhabitants of the said Parish.

Your Petitioners humbly pray your Lordship to consent to and confirm the proceedings of your Petitioners in this behalf, and grant to the Church Wardens of the said Parish of Horfield your Licence or Faculty to enable them to preserve and keep for the use of the Minister, Vestrymen and Inhabitants of the said Parish for the time being the said Parish church in its present state so already altered and enlarged with the addition of the said two wings And also your Lordship's sanction for the removal of the said tombstones and monuments and for replacing them in their original situations as aforesaid. And that the same may remain and continue in the same and with the like full benefit and advantage as if such Licence or Faculty had been obtained previously to the pulling down, rebuilding and enlarging of the said Church and the removal and replacement of the said tombstones and monuments. And your Petitioners will every pray etc.

| John Shadwell | Lay Rector | F K Barnes | } |
| Henry Richards | Minister | John Hember | } Inhabitants |
| John Bailey } | Churchwardens | Luke Williams | } |
| J. Marmont } | | Peregrine Rosling | } |

# Appendix 4

Photograph of 1846 faculty for the second enlargement of the church.

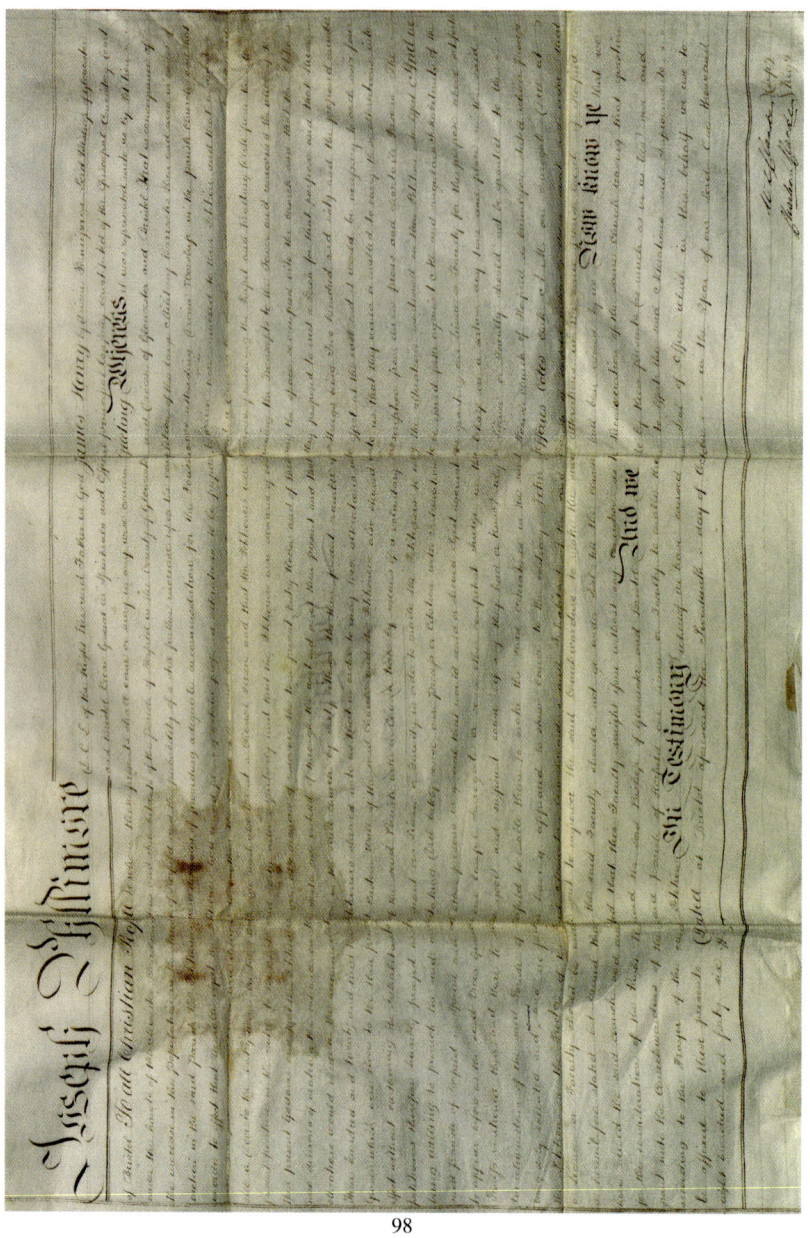

# Transcription of the 1847 faculty for the second enlargement of the church.

**Joseph Phillimore** DCL of the Right Reverend Father in God James Henry by Divine Permission Lord Bishop of Gloucester and Bristol Vicar General in Spirituals and Official Principal lawfully constituted of the Episcopal Consistory court of Bristol. To all Christian People to whom these presents shall come or may in any wise concern Greeting **Whereas** it was represented unto us by petition under the hands of the minister Churchwardens and Inhabitants of the parish of Horfield in the County of Gloucester and diocese of Gloucester and Bristol that in consequence of the increase in the population in the Parish of Horfield and the probability of a still further increase upon completion of the large military barracks then and now in course of erection in the said parish the petitioners were desirous of providing adequate accommodation for the parishioners attending Divine worship in the parish church and that in order to effect that desirable object the petitioners had caused plans of certain proposed alterations to be prepared which were annexed to their petition and that in accordance with such plans the petitioners were desirous to lengthen the chancel of the said church and to erect two windows and a door on the south side and one window on the north side also a door to the vestry room and also to erect a chancel screen and that the petitioners were desirous of removing the pulpit and reading desk from their their (sic) present positions in the centre to the North and south sides respectively and that the petitioners were desirous of continuing the transepts to the tower and removing the whole of their present galleries and that the petitioners were also desirous of removing the then present vestry room and of their throwing the space so occupied into the church and that the petitioners were desirous of making the entrance on the south side instead of through the west end as at their present and that they proposed to erect a porch for that purpose and that these alterations would increase the accommodation in the said church by sixty sittings the then present number of sittings being two hundred and sixty and the proposed number three hundred and twenty and that the petitioners showed unto us that in order to carry these alterations into effect at the east end it would be necessary to arch over four graves which were close to the then present eastern wall of the said church and the petitioners also showed unto us that they would be enabled to carry out these alterations into effect without burdening the inhabitants of the said parish with a church rate by means of a voluntary subscription from divers pious and charitable persons The petitioners therefore humbly prayed us to grant our licence or faculty in order to enable the petitioners to carry the alterations mentioned in their petition into effect. And we being willing to promote the said undertaking did lately cause our process or citation with invitation to be issued forth against all and singular inhabitants of the said parish of Horfield in special and all other persons in general that would could or should object against the granting our licence or faculty for the purposes above set forth to appear before us the said vicar general our lawful surrogate or some other competent judge in their behalf on a certain day time and place in the said process mentioned there and there to show good and sufficient cause (if any they had or knew) why a licence or faculty should not be granted to the churchwardens of the said parish of Horfield to allow them to make the said alterations in the parish of Horfield as hereinbefore stated which process being duly executed and returned and no person having appeared to show cause to the contrary John Jefferies Coles clerk A.M. our surrogate did at the petition of the proctor of the said Minister, churchwardens and inhabitants of the said parish of Horfield judicially decree direct and order that a licence of faculty should be made out to empower the said churchwardens to make the said alterations in the said parish church of Horfield as hereinbefore stated but decreed that the said faculty should not go under seal till the church had been viewed by us **Now know ye** that we have viewed the said church and directed that this faculty might issue without any condition as to reconsecration of the same church leaving that question for the consideration of the Right Reverend the Lord Bishop of Gloucester and Bristol **And we** do by these presents (as much as in us lies) give and grant unto the churchwardens of the said parish of Horfield our licence or faculty to enable them to effect the said alterations and improvements according to the prayer of the said petition **In Testimony** whereof we have caused our seal of office which is this behalf we use to be affixed to these presents Dated at Bristol aforesaid the seventeenth day of October in the year of our lord one thousand eight hundred and forty six.

                                                    W L Clarke    }Depy
                                                    Charles Clarke  }Regs

# Appendix 5

## The Church Building Today

The church as it stands today is described architecturally on the English Heritage website [47]. This description is incomplete in that it fails to mention the chapel on the South side of the chancel, St Andrew's Chapel, the clerestory on the South side of the nave roof and the window on the North side of the chancel. The descriptions of the windows are also minimal giving only details of the architectural styles and no details of the images within the windows. The information on the images and inscriptions in the windows is taken from the Horfield PCC archive.

The overall plan is cruciform with a West tower and a crossing tower. There is a chapel attached to the south side of the chancel and the choir vestry is attached to the North side of the chancel. There is a porch on the South side of the church and a former vestry attached to the north side of the tower at the west end of the church. The church is built in the Perpendicular style, except for the nave which is in the Decorated Gothic Revival-style.

Below is a photographic record of the exterior and interior as the church stands today. The pictures of the exterior go clockwise around the church beginning at the East end.

The chancel built in 1893 and to the left St Andrew's chapel, which was extended to its full length c 1913.

South side of Chapel and porch on East side of South Transept

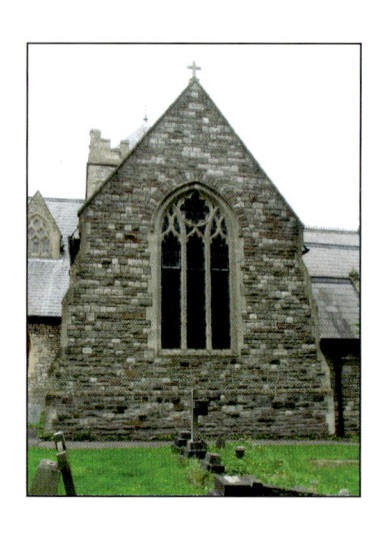

The South transept which was completed c 1920

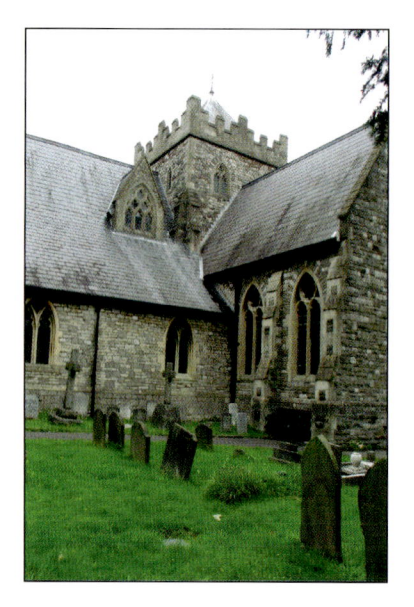

West wall of South transept and part of South aisle; South clerestory, c 1870, may be seen in nave roof near central tower, which was built in 1893.

South aisle, porch and tower at West end of church. The tower, which is c 15th century, is the oldest part of the standing church. The north and south aisles and the porch are all that remains of the 1847 enlargement of the church.

The West tower, the choir vestry, built in 1887 and North transept, which was built in 1929. The door in the base of the tower was inserted in 1836 as the main entrance to the church.

View of North side of church, showing tower, choir vestry, North clerestory, central tower and North transept.

Eastern most window in North aisle.

The central and western windows in the wall of the North aisle; stylistically the western window matches the eastern, see picture on right, but it is not known if it was installed at the same time.

North transept, which was built in 1929

Eastern side of North transept, showing octagonal external stair turret and ancillary buildings built in 1929. Between them and the chancel is the organ loft and sacristy, which was built in1893.Stairs lead down from the north wall of the chancel to a 'cellar' underneath.

Date stone on East wall of chancel.

Main door into church through porch on south side.

Roof of porch on the south side of the church.

Remains of window, c 15$^{th}$ century, in East wall of tower, blocked by the roof of the nave when the church was enlarged in 1847. The complete window is shown in the first known picture of the church.

## Fittings

Almost all of the fittings that were extant before 1893 are no longer in existence. These include the lower half of the wooden chancel screen, which was said by Bingham to have been medieval in date, the wooden pulpit used by Dr Edward Pusey, of the Oxford movement, when he preached at Horfield in the 1840s and an oak eagle lectern.

The font stands in the south transept, it is octagonal, made of stone, has tracery panels and is said to be of 16$^{th}$ century date[47]. It has a wooden cover with metal fittings.

There is an octagonal stone pulpit, at the north east corner of the crossing, it has a short shaft with open Tudor arches and Tudor roses, with iron-railed steps up. This is of early 20$^{th}$ century date being built to match the stone chancel screen that was erected at the time the south transept was constructed. This chancel screen was later removed.

Early 20$^{th}$ century octagonal stone pulpit, with stone steps and iron balustrade.

Octagonal stone font in South Transept, this is reported to be of 16$^{th}$ century date[47].

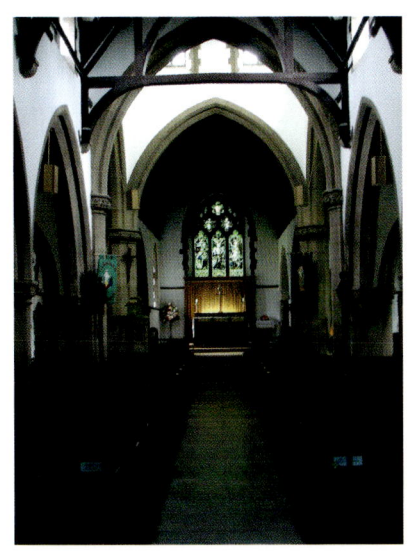

Looking East up the nave towards the chancel.

The width of the nave is the same as the width of the original church before any of the 19$^{th}$ and 20$^{th}$ century enlargements. Structurally the nave and the aisles have remained largely unaltered since 1847.

The chancel was enlarged to its current size in 1893. The white marble slab in the floor marks the position of the altar in the 1847 church. The arch to the side chapel was made in 1929.

Piscina built into the eastern side of the arch between the chancel and the side chapel. It was built in 1929. The left hand face is also pierced so that it is readily accessible from the main altar.

Carved capital on column in chancel; the carved capitals were part of the 1893 enlargement.

The side chapel, which in different documents is called St Andrew's Chapel or the Lady Chapel. It was built in 1893 and lengthened so that it became as long as the chancel in c1913.

The South transept was built c1920. It may be entered via a porch in the South-East corner. The war memorials for the First and Second World Wars are built into the East wall and East window of the transept, respectively. The font stands in the centre of the transept.

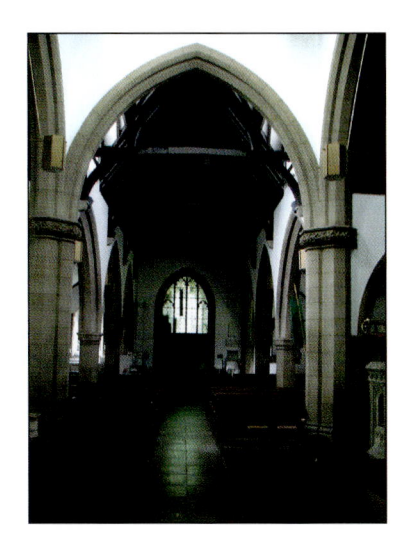

The North transept, this was built in 1929.

The pulpit may be seen by the right hand arch.

The Pye family vault lies, albeit filled in, beneath the left hand arch that leads to the nave. The Shadwell vault lies just beyond this arch under the western wall of the North transept. Other vaults probably also lie in this area but their positions are not known.

The ceiling of the crossing under the central lantern tower built in 1893

Looking down the nave to the West.

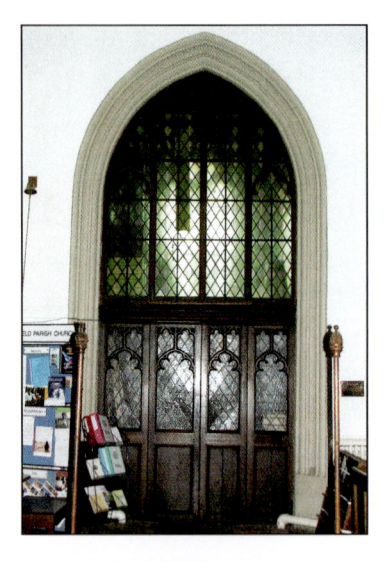

The West window; the date of the current window is unknown. There was no window in 1836 when the first floor of the tower was fitted with seats. These complemented galleries across the West end of the church and in the North and South transepts. At the time of the 1847 enlargement the seating and the galleries were removed. In Felix Farley's Journals description of the church following the work in 1847, it says that there was a window of painted glass.

The South and North aisles, were built in 1847 and remain unaltered. It is reported that the walls of the aisles were built before the old nave walls were taken down. At the West end of the North aisle is the window that was blocked when the choir vestry was built in 1887.

The door in the base of the tower. The doorway was inserted in 1836

Main door into church through South porch. This doorway was built in 1847.

# Windows

The descriptions of the windows go clockwise around the church beginning at the east window of the chancel. Only those that contain images or are of note are described. The remaining windows contain only plain or coloured glass.

## Chancel East Window behind the High Altar.

This is in the Decorated style with three lights. This window is shown in the chapter on memorials in the church.

Left hand light:        The Nativity,
Centre light:           The Crucifixion with Our Lady & St. John
Right hand light:       The Risen Lord with two Roman soldiers seated at his feet

In the tracery above are depicted two angels, and in a space at the top the figure of a priest robed in chasuble and alb and celebrating Mass.

At the base of the window an inscription which reads:

"In affectionate remembrance of Adelaide Mary Hutchinson, Died March 24th, 1908"

## East Window of Side Chapel, St Andrew's Chapel, behind the altar.

This is in the Decorated style with two lights

Left hand light:   St. Andrew,
Right hand light:  St. Peter,

At the base of the window is an inscription which reads: "He brought him to Jesus, St. John, 1, 40 — 43"

This window was present in the chapel before it was lengthened and was installed c1896 to commemorate Archibald Walters "The Boy Hero"

It is by Messrs. Heaton, Butler and Baines

## East window of the South transept.

This is in the Decorated style with two lights; it forms part of the Second World War memorial. It is shown in the chapter on memorials in the church.

Left hand light: St. Michael the Archangel with the badge of the Royal Air Force below the latter inscribed with the Motto: *Per Ardua ad Astra*
Right hand light: St. George with the badge of the British Army below
In the tracery above is a blue roundel bearing a naval crown.

It is noticeable that in the majority of the windows of the aisles the designs do not fit exactly in the windows. There is for example often a lack of symmetry at the bottom between the lights. This may suggest that the glass has been re-used from other windows.

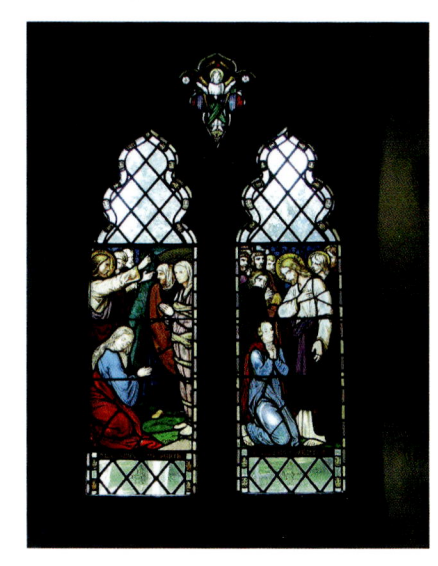

## Eastern window in South aisle.

This is in the Decorated style with two lights

Left hand light: The raising of Lazarus with the inscription "Lazarus come forth"

Beneath a small centrally placed clear diamond pane is inscribed
"Mary Elizabeth Richards, Died Sep. 7 1854,"

Right hand light: A woman touching Jesus' garment with the inscription "Jesus wept"

Beneath a small centrally placed clear diamond pane is inscribed
"Charles Henry Richards, Died Nov 29 1855,"

In the tracery at the top of the window is the figure of an angel with crossed wings in front.

Notice that the left hand margin of the picture in the left light is missing

## Western window in South aisle, near the porch.

This is in the Decorated style with two lights.

It consists of two coloured and patterned lights, with the figure of an angel with crossed wings in front in the tracery above.

## Western window in North aisle, nearest to the tower.

This is in the Decorated style with three lights, all with plain glass.

In two adjacent diamonds in the right hand-light an inscription has been written free-hand possibly using a diamond ring or similar. The inscription in the left hand of the two diamonds reads
"Susanna Howell Tintern Abbey nr Chepstow  Mon"
The inscription in the adjacent right hand diamond reads
" Miss   Green    Miss Pincombe Bristol".

To date it has not been possible to find out who these women were and why and/or when they wrote on the glass.

114

## Middle window in North aisle.

This is in the Decorated style with two lights.

The two lights depict the raising of Jairus' daughter, and below is the inscription "Weep not, she is not dead but sleepeth"

## Eastern window in North aisle, nearest to the organ.

This is in the Decorated style with three lights.

The two outer lights are of coloured and patterned glass.
The centre light depicts Jesus surrounded by children with the figure of St, Peter behind him holding a key in his left hand.

At the base is the inscription "Jesus said suffer the little children to come unto Me and forbid them not for of such is ye kingdom of Heaven and He took them up in His arms, He laid His hands upon them and blessed them"

This window best exemplifies how the glass in the aisle windows often does not fit exactly.

## East window in Choir Vestry.

This is a two-light window in the Decorated style with tracery above.

The glass in the lights is plain. There are three figures of angels in the tracery above.

## West Wall of Tower in the first stage.

This is a two light window in the Decorated style.

The glass in each of the lights is plain, but in the tracery above are the figures of two angels.

# Glossary

Aumbrey: A closed recess in a church for holding books and sacred utensils.

Canon: The metal loop or 'ear' at the top of a bell, by which it is hung.

Capella   Chapel

Capital: The top or head of a column.

Chancel: Eastern part of a church containing the choir and main altar.

Chapelry: A division of a large or populous parish which has its own chapel.

Chartist: Chartists mainly wanted a much wider franchise with secret ballots etc.

Chasuble: A long sleeveless vestment worn by a priest when celebrating mass. It is worn over the alb, which is a long white linen vestment with sleeves.

Clerestory: A window or row of windows set up high in the walls of a church or the roof.

Copyhold Land: A form of medieval tenure for life.

Decorated: A rich ornamental style of English Gothic architecture in use from c 1275 to 1380

Deed of Gift: A transfer of an owner's property to another person where no payment is demanded in return.

Early English: The first period of English Gothic architecture in use from c 1180 to 1275, it is characterised by the pointed arch known as the lancet.

Encaustic Tiles: Earthenware tiles patterned with inlays of coloured clay slips.

Faculty: A faculty is a legal instrument or warrant in church law, from an ecclesiastical court or tribunal. A church petitions, for a faculty to carry out certain works and then the ecclesiastical court or tribunal will decide if a faculty should be issued. It may be issued with conditions attached to it.

| | |
|---|---|
| Hundred: | An early division of land, predating division by counties. |
| Incumbent: | The priest in charge of a parish |
| Inverse Arch: | An "up-side down" arch used in the foundations to provide support to the structure above. |
| Lancet window: | A tall narrow window, terminating in a narrow pointed arch. |
| Lantern tower: | A tower placed over the junction of the cross formed by the nave, transepts and chancel. There are usually windows in each face of the tower. |
| Light: | The vertical sections of a window either side of a mullion. A mullion is a vertical stone bar that runs from the tracery at the top of the window to the bottom. |
| Nave: | The body of the church, the area extending westwards from the transepts to the entrance. It is the area where the congregation sits. |
| Perpendicular: | The final phase of English Gothic architecture in use from c 1380 to 1520. |
| Piscina: | Stone basin with a drain used for washing sacred vessels; usually located on the South side of the church. |
| Prebend: | The revenue of a specific plot of land belonging to an ecclesiastical foundation, usually an abbey or cathedral; a *prebendary* was the priest to which a prebend was allocated. |
| Romanesque: | The style of architecture introduced after the Norman Conquest in use from c 1066-1180. |
| Sedilid (sic): | Sedilia, the seats inside the chancel, used by officiating clergy |
| Tracery: | The ornamental curved stonework in Gothic windows. |
| Transept: | The transepts are the arms of the church that project North and South from the nave at the point where it joins the chancel. |

# References

1. http://www.hrionline.ac.uk/taxatio/info.html - this is a web link to the project that is aiming to catalogue and transcribe the original records. It also explains some of the background to the *taxatio*.
2. Taylor, C.S., Berkeley Minster, TBGAS-Online **19** (1894-95) 70-84
3. Dawson,D., Archaeology and the Medieval Churches of Bristol, BARG Review **2** (1981) 9-24
4. Sabin, A., St. Augustine's Abbey and the Berkeley Churches, TBGAS-Online **89** (1970) 90-98
5. Register of Bishop Carpenter, part 2 (1467-1476), entry is dated 29 May 1472, appears in folio 43 (modern pages 105-106), Worcester Record Office ref. b716.093 Acc.2648/6b(iii) fol.43
6. Will of John Walter 1502, Canterbury Cathedral ref. Register F fo. 262v
7. Photocopy of extract from *Valor Ecclesiasticus*, (Original is in PRO), Gloucestershire Record Office, ref D1120
8. *Valor Ecclesiasticus*, The Record Commission transcript (printed between 1810-1834), a copy is held at Gloucester Record Office.
9. Lindley, E.S., A Short Study in Valor Ecclesiasticus, TBGAS-Online **76** (1957) 98-117
10. Seyer's Map of Horfield, Bristol Record Office, ref. P.Hor/X/1
11. Plan of Horfield Rectory Site, Bristol Record Office, ref. P/HOR/I/10 (a)
12. Horfield Tithe Map, Bristol Record Office, ref. EP-A-32-23
13. Bingham, F., Horfield Miscellanea, Pub. W.H. Barrell, Portsmouth [1905], available at Bristol Reference Library
14. Quotation for building rectory at Horfield, Gloucestershire Record Office, ref. GDR/G2/3/Box 1/14677
15. Wright, D., Population in Horfield 1066-1851, Research Group Paper 1, Pub. Bishopton Horfield & Ashley Down Local History Society (2007)
16. Horfield, (Holy Trinity) (1836-1837) Gloucestershire, ICBS Minutes, Volume 8, pages 26, 100, 119, also ICBS 01958 Folios 29ff, available at Lambeth Palace Library
17. Faculty for enlargement in 1836 and associated drawings/plans; Bristol Record Office, ref. EP/J/6/1
18. Leech, J. The church-goer: rural rides, or calls at country churches, second series, $2^{nd}$ edn, Pub. John Ridler (1850), at Bristol Reference Library
19. Horfield, (Holy Trinity) (1847-1849) Gloucestershire, ICBS Minutes, Volume 13, pages 54, 82 also ICBS 03959, available at Lambeth Palace Library
20. Copies of all the Felix Farley's Journals and the Bristol Times & Mirror quoted are held at Bristol Reference Library
21. Faculty for enlargement in1847 and associated plans & drawings, Bristol Record Office, ref. P-Hor-CLW-2(a) and EP/J/6/2/141

| | |
|---|---|
| 22. | Faculty for re-consecration following enlargement in 1847, Bristol Record Office, ref. EP/A/22/Hor/1a-c |
| 23. | Consistory Court Records, 1840-1849, Bristol Record Office, ref. EP/A/45/3 |
| 24. | Horfield PCC Church Archive |
| 25. | Faculty for building new vestry room and organ chamber, Bristol Record Office, P/Hor/Chw/2/b |
| 26. | Horfield vestry minutes 1847-1876, Bristol Record Office, ref. P/Hor/V/1 |
| 27. | Fanshaw Bingham's research notes, Bristol Record Office, ref. P/Hor/X/2 |
| 28. | Horfield vestry minutes 1877-1847, Bristol Record Office, ref. P/Hor/V/2 |
| 29. | The only known plan and drawing for the worked completed in 1887 is held in private hands in Bristol. |
| 30. | Drawings and plans relating to period 1884-1893, Bristol Record Office, ref. EP/J/6/2/141 |
| 31. | Horfield, (Holy Trinity) (1884-1894) Gloucestershire, ICBS Minutes, Volume 26, pages 86, 108, 311, Volume 29, page 169, also ICBS 09358, available at Lambeth Palace Library |
| 32. | Faculty for work to be carried out in 1893, Bristol Record Office, ref. EP/J/6/2/141 |
| 33. | Faculty for re-consecration of church in 1893, Bristol Record Office, ref.: EP/J/6/2/141 |
| 34. | Drawings and plans for proposed 1911 building work, Bristol Record Office, EP/J/6/2/141 also P/Hor/P/5(a-d) |
| 35. | Faculty for work for original proposals to build transepts in 1911, Bristol Record Office, P.Hor/Chw/2/d |
| 36. | Drawings for proposed 1929 building works, Bristol Record Office, ref. P/Hor/P/5(a-d) |
| 37. | Faculty for building North transept and other works, Bristol Record Office, ref. P/Hor/Chw/2/g |
| 38. | Licence to perform divine service At St Edmunds during repairs to parish church, with covering letter, dated 5th October 1929, Bristol Record Office P/Hor/I/7(c) |
| 39. | Licence to perform divine service At Edmund's Trust National Boys' School, parish church accommodation being inadequate, dated 14th November 1905, Bristol Record Office, ref. P/Hor/I/7/a |
| 40. | Record of overspend on repairs and maintenance on church, Bristol Record Office, P/Hor/Chw/10 |
| 41. | Licence to perform divine service In Church Hall, during repairs to parish church, dated 18th November 1944, Bristol Record Office, ref. P/Hor/I/7(e) |
| 42 | Picture of medieval stained glass from Horfield parish church, http://www.cvma.ac.uk/index.html, ref 007194 |
| 43. | Bigland, Ralph, Historical, monumental and genealogical collections relative to the County of Gloucester, Part 2, Daglington-Moreton Valence, edited by Brian Frith, Gloucestershire Record Series vol. 3, Pub. Alan |

|     | Sutton for Bristol & Gloucestershire Archaeological Society (1990) This is a facsimile reprint of the original printed in London in c 1791-92. It is available at Bristol Reference Library and Bristol Record Office. |
|-----|---|
| 44. | Letters of Fanshawe Bingam, these contain a lot of interesting information about the building works, construction, his personal views on some of the later work that was carried out etc., Bristol Record Office P/Hor/I/23/2 |
| 45. | Wright, D., Horfield Parish Registers of Baptisms, Burials and Marriages 1543 - 1812, Research Group Paper 3, Pub. Bishopton Horfield & Ashley Down Local History Society (2007) |
| 46. | Faculty to level graves and move head stones, dated 1967, Bristol Record Office, ref. P/Hor/Chw/2/l |
| 47. | http://www.imagesofengland.org.uk – search for Horfield Church |
| 48. | Information on organ courtesy of Bristol & District Organists' Association |

Previous books in the series:

Population in Horfield 1066-1851     ISBN 978-0-9555826-1-5

The Horfield Tithe Survey 1841       ISBN 978-0-9555826-0-8

Horfield Parish Registers of Baptisms,
Burials and Marriages 1543 – 1812    ISBN 978-0-9555826-2-2